Dispossession:
The Performative
in the Political

Dispossession: The Performative in the Political

Conversations with
Athena Athanasiou

Judith Butler

polity

First published in 2013 by Polity Press
Reprinted 2013 (four times), 2014 (three times), 2015 (three times),
2017, 2018, 2020, 2021

Polity Press
65 Bridge Street
Cambridge CB2 1UR, UK

Polity Press
350 Main Street
Malden, MA 02148, USA

ISBN-13: 978-0-7456-5380-8
ISBN-13: 978-0-7456-5381-5(pb)

A catalogue record for this book is available from the British Library.

Typeset in 11 on 14 pt Sabon
by Toppan Best-set Premedia Limited
Printed and bound by CPI Group (UK) Ltd, Croydon, CR0 4YY

The publisher has used its best endeavours to ensure that the URLs for
external websites referred to in this book are correct and active at the time
of going to press. However, the publisher has no responsibility for the
websites and can make no guarantee that a site will remain live or that the
content is or will remain appropriate.

Every effort has been made to trace all copyright holders, but if any have
been inadvertently overlooked the publisher will be pleased to include any
necessary credits in any subsequent reprint or edition.

For further information on Polity, visit our website: www.politybooks.com

Contents

Contents

Preface

The two of us met in Athens, Greece, in December 2009, when Judith gave the Nicos Poulantzas Memorial Lecture for the Poulantzas Institute, affiliated with SYRIZA (Coalition of the Radical Left), and spoke for the Department of Social Anthropology at the Panteion University, where Athena is a professor. We began a conversation on politics, theory, embodiment, and new formations of left politics, focused at first on the question of how older left politics might respond to newer feminist and queer concerns with resisting precarity. Our first conversation (which was published in Greek), "Questioning the Normative, Reconfiguring the Possible: Feminism, Queer Politics and the Radical Left," appeared in the volume *Performativity and Precarity: Judith Butler in Athens* (Athens: nissos, 2011).[1]

Athena's own work focuses on feminist theory and radical social thought, bringing perspectives on the work of Luce Irigaray and Michel Foucault to critically consider critically relations between masculinism, technology, and the human. Athena's volume, co-edited with

Elena Tzelepis, *Rewriting Difference: Luce Irigaray and the "Greeks"* (Albany: SUNY Press, 2010), moves from tropes derived from classical Greek myth to contemporary transnational and postcolonial contexts of corporeal and critical practices. She has published a book in Greek called *Life at the Limit: Essays on the Body, Gender, and Biopolitics* (Athens: Ekkremes, 2007),[2] in which she offers a post-human and post-Lacanian psychoanalytic account of technology, difference, embodiment, and bodies of knowledge, focusing on how they inform the contemporary social organization of livability, desire, and gendered and sexual subjectivity. She has also written a book (*Crisis as a "State of Exception": Critiques and Resistances*, Athens: Savvalas, 2012)[3] on the bodily dimensions of the Greek debt crisis; in it she addresses the indefinite state of exception as an instance of neoliberal governmental rationality conducted in the name of the economic emergency and involving forces of racialization and feminization that fundamentally structure the condition of "becoming precarious." Her overall work focuses on forms of queer deconstruction and feminist modes of performative politics, including non-violent public demonstrations of grieving and resistance to contemporary regimes of biopolitics, such as the work of the transnational, antimilitaristic, feminist movement Women in Black. In considering concrete manifestations of subversive gender performativity, Athena has been inspired by Judith's philosophical work on ethics and politics, gender and queer performativity, corporeality, language, normative violence and violence of derealization, the vulnerability of human life and the question of what makes for a livable life. And Judith has been challenged by Athena's anthropological and philosophical perspectives wrought from Irigaray and Heidegger as well as the geopolitical challenges of neoliberalism that have been so acutely registered in Greece. Like Judith, Athena has been engaging with a non-sovereign account of agency, the relationality of the self, freedom with others, questions of recognition and desire, as well as the gendered, sexual, and racial implications of one's bodily exposure to one another. So our conversation insistently explored these questions, as we sought to convey and map out the political and affective labor of critical agency.

Our conversation began with the consideration of a poststructuralist position we both share, namely that the idea of the unitary subject serves a form of power that must be challenged and undone, signifying a style of masculinism that effaces sexual difference and enacts mastery over the domain of life. We recognized that both of us thought that ethical and political responsibility emerges only when a sovereign and unitary subject can be effectively challenged, and that the fissuring of the subject, or its constituting "difference," proves central for a politics that challenges both property and sovereignty in specific ways. Yet as much as we prize the forms of responsibility and resistance that emerge from a "dispossessed" subject – one that *avows* the differentiated social bonds by which it is constituted and to which it is obligated – we also were keenly aware that dispossession constitutes a form of suffering for those displaced and colonized and so could not remain an unambivalent political ideal. We started to think together about how to formulate a theory of political performativity that could take into account the version of dispossession that we valued as well as the version we oppose.

The following represents a wide-ranging dialogue that happened over several months in meetings, conversations, and writing, but mainly on email, though we met in London in February 2011 to plot the trajectory of this exchange. During that meeting in London, the Egyptian revolution was in full swing, and in the last weeks of writing this text together the Greek Left posed a serious challenge to the neoliberal politics of austerity, opening up the possibility of a new European Left opposed to the differential distribution of precarity and the technocratic suppression of democracy. Our reflections register these events obliquely, and in the course of this exchange we refer to several political movements, demonstrations, and acts that helped us to formulate what we mean by a politics of the performative. Our approaches converge and differ. Athena's geopolitical position informs her reflections on modes of resistance and public mourning, and she draws from the work of Irigaray, Heidegger's critique of technology, Foucault's notion of biopolitics, and post-Lacanian psychoanalysis.[4] Judith's work emerges from Foucault and speech act theory, gender theory, queer activism, and heterodox psychoanalysis. Both of us return to Greek myths to understand the present, which means that those myths are animated in new ways, as in an extraordinary film that we discuss, *Strella* (dir. Panos Koutras, 2009), in which a transgendered sex worker lives out a contemporary Oedipal myth in twenty-first-century Athens. Along the way, we seek in convergent ways to prepare Hannah Arendt for a Left she would not have joined, and we enter into questions of affect and ethics within the frame of politics by thinking through recent forms of political mobilization.

Both of us found ourselves returning to the question, "What makes political responsiveness possible?" The predicament of being moved by what one sees, feels, and comes to know is always one in which one finds oneself transported elsewhere, into another scene, or into a social world in which one is not the center. And this form of dispossession is constituted as a form of responsiveness that gives rise to action and resistance, to appearing together with others, in an effort to demand the end of injustice. One form that injustice takes is the systematic dispossession of peoples through, for example, forced migration, unemployment, homelessness, occupation, and conquest. And so we take up the question of how to become dispossessed of the sovereign self and enter into forms of collectivity that oppose forms of dispossession that systematically jettison populations from modes of collective belonging and justice.

June 2012, Berkeley and Athens

I

Aporetic dispossession, or the trouble with dispossession

AA: Dispossession is a troubling concept. It is so troubling that as we seek to write about it, it is highly possible that it gets us into trouble. In order to put this troubling concept to work – that is, in order to engage with the ways in which it gets us in trouble – we must confront an aporia. On the one side, dispossession signifies an inaugural submission of the subject-to-be to norms of intelligibility, a submission which, in its paradoxical simultaneity with mastery, constitutes the ambivalent and tenuous processes of subjection. It thus resonates with the psychic foreclosures that determine which "passionate attachments" are possible and plausible for "one" to become a subject. In this sense, dispossession encompasses the constituted, preemptive losses that condition one's being dispossessed (or letting oneself become dispossessed) by another: one is moved to the other and by the other – exposed to and affected by the other's vulnerability. The subject comes to "exist" by installing within itself lost objects along with the social norms that regulate the subject's disposition to the address of the other. On the other side (the extent to which this side can be assumed as "other" will have to remain in suspension for a while), being dispossessed refers to processes and ideologies by which persons are disowned and abjected by normative and normalizing powers that define cultural intelligibility and that regulate the distribution of vulnerability: loss of land and community; ownership of one's living body by another person, as in histories of slavery; subjection to military, imperial, and economic violence; poverty, securitarian regimes, biopolitical subjectivation, liberal possessive individualism, neoliberal governmentality, and precaritization.

If in the first sense dispossession stands as a heteronomic condition for autonomy, or, perhaps more accurately, as a limit to the autonomous and impermeable self-sufficiency of the liberal subject through its injurious yet enabling fundamental dependency and relationality, in the second sense dispossession implies imposed injuries, painful interpellations, occlusions, and foreclosures, modes of subjugation that call to be addressed and redressed. In the first sense, avowing the trace of primary passions and losses – as one's psychic and social attachment to the law that determines one's disposition to alterity – is a necessary condition of the subject's survival; in the second sense, dispossession is a condition painfully imposed by the normative and normalizing violence that determines the terms of subjectivity, survival, and livability. In both senses, dispossession involves the subject's relation to norms, its mode of becoming by means of assuming and resignifying injurious interpellations and impossible passions. The task here, a task of gesturing to the performative in the political, is to weave the two valences of dispossession together and to perform this interweaving of the two valences beyond and counter to the logic of numeration and calculability; rather than ordering attributes into a coherent and fixed sequence, then, we should gesture to what resists assimilation into the framework of dispossession.

JB: It is true that dispossession carries this double valence and that as a result it is difficult to understand until we see that we value it in one of its modalities and abhor and resist it in another. As you say, dispossession can be a term that marks the limits of self-sufficiency and that establishes us as relational and interdependent beings. Yet dispossession is precisely what happens when populations lose their land, their citizenship, their means of livelihood, and become subject to military and legal violence. We oppose this latter form of dispossession because it is both forcible and privative. In the first sense, we are dispossessed of ourselves by virtue of some kind of contact with another, by virtue of being moved and even surprised or disconcerted by that encounter with alterity. The experience itself is not simply episodic, but can and does reveal one basis of relationality – we do not simply move ourselves, but are ourselves moved by what is outside us, by others, but also by whatever "outside" resides in us. For instance, we are moved by others in ways that disconcert, displace, and dispossess us; we sometimes no longer know precisely who we are, or by what we are driven, after contact with some other or some other group, or as a result of someone else's actions. One can be dispossessed in grief or in passion

– unable to find oneself. Much of Greek tragedy relies on this undoing of self-sufficient forms of deliberation, the dispossessions of grief, love, rage, ambition, ecstasy. These forms of experience call into question whether we are, as bounded and deliberate individuals, self-propelling and self-driven. Indeed, they suggest that we are moved by various forces that precede and exceed our deliberate and bounded selfhood. As such, we cannot understand ourselves without in some ways giving up on the notion that the self is the ground and cause of its own experience. A number of postulates follow: we can say that dispossession establishes the self as social, as passionate, that is, as driven by passions it cannot fully consciously ground or know, as dependent on environments and others who sustain and even motivate the life of the self itself.

The second sense of dispossession is bound to the first. For if we are beings who can be deprived of place, livelihood, shelter, food, and protection, if we can lose our citizenship, our homes, and our rights, then we are fundamentally dependent on those powers that alternately sustain or deprive us, and that hold a certain power over our very survival. Even when we have our rights, we are dependent on a mode of governance and a legal regime that confers and sustains those rights. And so we are already outside of ourselves before any possibility of being dispossessed of our rights, land, and modes of belonging. In other words, we are inter-dependent beings whose pleasure and suffering depend from the start on a sustained social world, a sustaining environment. This does not mean that everyone is born into a sustaining world. Not at all. But when someone is born into malnutrition or physical exposure or some other condition of extreme precarity, we see precisely how the deprivation of that sustaining world can and does thwart or vanquish a life. So every life is in this sense outside itself from the start, and its "dispossession" in the forcible or privative sense can only be understood against that background. We can only be dispossessed because we are already dispossessed. Our interdependency establishes our vulnerability to social forms of deprivation.

AA: I agree with you that "we can only be dispossessed because we are already dispossessed," as you put it, but I am also hesitating. My sense is that language may fail us here insofar as such a formulation contrives to establish a causal link between "being" dispossessed, on the one side, and "becoming" or "being made" dispossessed, on the other. Although the two senses of dispossession are bound to each other, there is no ontological, causal, or chronological link between "being dispossessed" (as a primordial disposition to relationality that lies at a fundamental level of subjection and signals a constitutive self-displacement, that is, the constitution of the subject through certain kinds of foreclosure and preemptive loss) and "becoming dispossessed" (as an ensuing, derivative condition of enforced deprivation of land, rights, livelihood, desire, or modes of belonging). We should be wary of conflating or ontologically demarcating these nuances of dispossession. In fact, one of our efforts in this intervention ought to be to seek to denaturalize and repoliticize the ways in which "being always already dispossessed" is often summoned to legitimize an abdication of political responsibility for social forms of deprivation and dispossession.

————

There is a very complicated affective, psychic, and political dynamic involved in the multiple nuances of "becoming dispossessed," one that takes us to the multi-layered traumas of subjection and the foreclosures that structure our "passionate attachments," the fore-closures that produce melancholia in determining which passionate attachments are possible and viable, and which are not (for instance the disavowal of same-sex desire). How do we think these two modes of dispos-session together? Moreover, how does this double valence of dispossession relate violent foreclosures of gender and sexuality with convergent troubling issues of our time such as statelessness, racism, poverty, xeno-phobia, and ensuing modalities of exposure to violence and recourse to rights?

The notion of dispossession, in all its intractable ways of signaling the contemporary production of social dis-courses, modes of power, and subjects, is a theoretical trope that might help us begin to address the fact that dis-possession carries the presumption that someone has been deprived of something that rightfully belongs to them. In this sense, dispossession is also akin to the Marxist concept of alienation, which works on two levels: laboring subjects are deprived of the ability to have control over their life, but they are also denied the consciousness of their subjugation as they are interpel-lated as subjects of inalienable freedom. At the same time, it is equally important to think about disposses-sion as a condition that is not simply countered by appropriation, a term that re-establishes possession and property as the primary prerogatives of self-authoring personhood. The challenge that we face here, and it is a simultaneously ethical, political, and theoretical challenge, is double. Firstly, we must elaborate on how to think about dispossession outside of the logic of possession (as a hallmark of modernity, liberalism, and humanism), that is, not only avoiding but also calling into question the exclusionary calculus of proprietariness in late liberal forms of power; and, secondly, we must elaborate why this reflective gesture is politically significant.

JB: Yes, and to this end, we might wonder why certain forms of human deprivation and exploitation are called "dispossession." Was there a property that was first owned and then was stolen? Sometimes, yes. Yet, what do we make of the idea that we have property in our own persons? Are persons forms of property, and would we be able to understand this legal formulation at all if it were not for the historical conditions of slavery and those forms of possessive individualism that belong to capitalism? It seems to me that MacPherson gave us an important genealogy of the production of the possessive individual, one which effectively claims that where there is no possession of property, there is no individual.[1] So I see us as working against this key construct of capitalism at the same time as we object to forms of land theft and territorial dispossession. This leads me to wonder whether we can find ethical and political ways of objecting to forcible and coercive dispossession that do not depend upon a valorization of possessive individualism.

AA: Exactly. This is a question that reflects our attempt to critically engage with the various discursive, subjective, institutional, and affective formations of late liberal reason in national and global contexts. It is in this perspective that we must focus on discursive and performative regimes of dispossession as well as on critical responses to them. And it is in this perspective that we need to object to forcible regimes of dispossession in contexts of liberal governmentality, where "owning" always denotes "possessive individualism."

JB: Those forms of moral philosophy that ground their objections to land theft on the rights of the individual to property very often deflect from the colonial conditions, for instance, under which property is systematically confiscated. Indeed, one would not be able to understand or even object to property theft in Israel/Palestine without understanding the function of the confiscation of Palestinian lands since 1948 as part of settler colonialism and the founding of the nation-state on principles of Jewish sovereignty. So though in every instance of land confiscation a person's land was taken, and that "person" remains a singular and irreducible one, it is equally true that everyone who lost her or his lands through these forcible means (750,000 in 1948 alone) is implicated in processes of colonization and state formation. In other words, we cannot understand what happens to an individual's land if we do not understand both the social form of property and the social form of individuality.

Those who ground their objections on the basis of the claims of possessive individualism tend to argue that an individual owns land by virtue of laboring on it, or by virtue of a contract that compels recognition of that claim of ownership. In the early years of Zionism, it was clear that Jews invoked Lockean principles to claim that because they worked the land and established irrigation networks, this laboring activity implied rights of ownership, even rights of national belonging grounded on territory. We can see how, in fact, the aims of both the nation and the colony depended upon an ideology of possessive individualism that was recast as possessive nationalism.

In Palestine, deeds to property and explicit legal contracts were regularly disregarded in the name of national interest. Similarly, the labor theory of value was actually invoked by Zionists to counter claims of existing contracts and deeds. So the question is not whether possessive individualism is a good or a bad ontology; rather, the question is how it works, and in the service of what sorts of political aims. If we question the "desire to possess" as a natural property of individuals, then we can, as MacPherson does, begin to ask the historical question of how the desire to possess property on an individual basis was produced over time as a natural, if not essential, characteristic of human personhood, and for what purposes. From a philosophical point of view, we can then ask, as well, whether this production of possessive individualism depended upon a disavowal of more primary social, dependent, and relational modes of existence. In the case of Palestine, we can ask how systematic land confiscation undermines the legal and economic conditions of cohabitation. In this sense, the privative form of dispossession makes the relational form of dispossession impossible. I think this comes close to what you mean, Athena, by the heteronomic condition of autonomy.

2

The logic of dispossession and the matter of the human (after the critique of metaphysics of substance)

AA: In general, dispossession speaks to how human bodies become materialized and de-materialized through histories of slavery, colonization, apartheid, capitalist alienation, immigration and asylum politics, post-colonial liberal multiculturalism, gender and sexual normativity, securitarian governmentality, and humanitarian reason.

It might be helpful to consider that in the proper sense of the word, if such a thing exists, "dispossession" originally referred to practices of land encroachment. Colonial and racist assumptions have been historically mobilized to justify and naturalize the misrecognition, appropriation, and occupation of indigenous lands in colonial and postcolonial settler contexts – such as in the case of the dispossession of indigenous people and the occupation of Palestinian lands and resources by the Israeli state. In such contexts, either by means of national monoculturalism, liberal multicultural (mis)recognition, biopiracy, and reification of "cultural diversity," or apartheid, such as the separation wall in Palestine, dispossession works as an authoritative and often paternalistic apparatus of controlling and appropriating the spatiality, mobility, affectivity, potentiality, and relationality of (neo-)colonized subjects. In such contexts, "dispossession" offers language to express experiences of uprootedness, occupation, destruction of homes and social bonds, incitation to "authentic" self-identities, humanitarian victimization, unlivability, and struggles for self-determination.[1]

The formation of prevailing assumptions about what constitutes land as colonial settler space, sovereign nation-state territory, or bourgeois private property lies at the heart of the history of western modern human subjectivity. In today's global market economy of neoliberal capitalism and "debtocracy,"[2] dispossession signifies the violent appropriation of labor and the wearing out of laboring and non-laboring bodies. This has manifested in the current politics of economic precarity in the form of temporary, low-paying, and insecure jobs, in combination with cuts to welfare provision and expropriation of public education and health institutions. International financial institutions prescribe to indebted countries measures of austerity (such as cutting public expenditures) as prerequisites for loans. Through neoliberal austerity measures, the governments of European nation-states protect market sovereignty and banks while attacking the lowest-paid workers, the unemployed, the urban poor, and the impoverished urban middle classes. Common, collective, and public assets are converted into private property rights. This redistributive politics is relevant to what David Harvey has described as the neoliberal drive toward "accumulation by dispossession."[3] In neoliberal frames of privatization, financialization, and management of crises, jobs are being taken away, hopes are obliterated, and bodies are instrumentalized and worn out. But new life forms and forms of subjectivity are also being produced (that is, human life turned into capital), as "debt" becomes a fundamental technology of biopolitical governmentality – a political and moral economy of life itself. This is, in fact, the original meaning of "economy": the allotment and management of the *oikos* (the house, the household) as the site par excellence of human capital. This etymology is very suggestive of the current shift taking place in the domain of power, from the rule of law and the production of the ordinary to measures of crisis-management and therapeutic decrees of emergency (which, in turn, inculcate another order of ordinariness).

In such contexts of knowledge, power, and subjectivity, it is worth rethinking democracy, citizenship, and collective agency by means of developing new political strategies that engage the dispossession of indebtedness as a crucial moment in the histories of liberal western governmentality. Land and property ownership has surely been at the heart of the onto-epistemologies of subject formation in the histories of the western, white, male, colonizing, capitalist, property-owning, sovereign human subject. In the political imaginary of (post)colonial capitalist western modernity and its claims of universal humanity, being and having are constituted as ontologically akin to each other; being is defined as having; having is constructed as an essential prerequisite of proper human being.[4] Also, the definition of the ownership of one's body as property is a founding moment of liberalism. However, certain bodies – paradigmatically so the bodies of slaves – are excluded from this classic definition of the biopolitical, which forges a constitutive connection between life, ownership, and liberty.

JB: Yes, but perhaps we have to be careful about how we differentiate these particular histories. After all, there may be many political imaginaries of "the West," and "the West" is surely also a function of a political imaginary itself. But you are suggesting, rightly, that property relations have come to structure and control our moral concepts of personhood, self-belonging, agency, and self-identity. Perhaps you approach through a slightly different language the problem of self-sufficiency that I suggest above. For you, it seems, this relation of a self to itself is described as "self-presence" and is itself implicated in a metaphysics of presence. I wonder whether presence can be distinguished from self-identity and even self-sufficiency. If we are, for instance, "present" to one another, we may be dispossessed by that very presence. Is this at least a possibility for you? It seems to me that there is a presence implied by the idea of bodily exposure, which can become the occasion of subjugation or acknowledgement. The coercive exposure of bodies at checkpoints or other sites of intensified surveillance can be one instance of the former. The body must arrive, present itself for inspection, and move only according to the motion and speed required by the soldier or the machine (or the soldier–machine hybrid). We can say that at these instances the person who must pass through the checkpoint is "present" in a way that is bound up with subjugation. But similarly, when acts of resistance happen at the checkpoint, when bodies show up or move through in ways that are not allowed, or when communities form on either side to limit and counter military practices, a kind of presence occurs. How do we think about these more ordinary forms of being or making present in light of the metaphysical category of presence that you work with here?

AA: It is true that I am interested in ways we could think of the forces of dispossession in late liberal contexts without retreating into the metaphysics of presence. Now, I take it that your question concerns the vexed thematics of agency. Similarly, the question for me is how we might tackle the problematic of agency by drawing on post-essentialist thought and without reiterating the terms set by liberal imaginaries and normativities. So, the fact that "presence" can never quite be disengaged from the metaphysical conceits of self-identity, self-sufficiency, and self-transparency does not mean that it is always already subsumed by these conceits. Presence, in its modality of *becoming* present to one another, can be an occasion of critical displacement. So yes, in becoming present to one another, we may be dispossessed by that very presence. In becoming present to one another, as an occasion of being both bound up with subjugation and responsive and receptive to others, we may be positioned within and against the authoritative order of presence that produces and constrains the intelligibility of human or non-human presence. Acts of resistance will take established orders of subjection as their resource, but they are not condemned to hopelessly reproducing or enhancing these orders. "Self-presence" is an attachment to an injurious interpellation, which becomes the condition of possibility for non-normative resignifications of what matters as presence. Even though the metaphysics of presence is not something that can be evaded or thwarted at will, this does not mean that we cannot be present to one another in ways not subsumed by this order. Even though we are compelled to reiterate the norms by which we are produced as present subjects, this very reiteration poses a certain risk, for if we reinstate presence in a different, or catachrestic way, we might put our social existence at risk (that is, we risk desubjectivization). But we might also start to performatively displace and reconfigure the contours of what matters, appears, and can be assumed as one's own intelligible presence. Now, might such a catachrestic repetition that turns presence against its hegemonic modes be assumed as "one's own" by the standards of possessive and privative individualism? I don't think so. My sense is that acts of agency, as effects of performativity, cannot be assumed as "one's own." In the spirit of indeterminate performativity, however, acts of catachrestic "making present" often displace the terms (that is, including property, priority, and propriety) by which presence has attained its normative omnipresence, as it were.

Your reference to the coercive exposure of bodies at sites of intensified surveillance is certainly very suggestive in that respect. I remember, a few years ago, an anti-occupation demonstration organized by Women in Black at the infamous Qalandiya checkpoint, a military crossing established by Israel to control the movement of people between Ramallah and the divided city of Jerusalem. People were forced to wait in the burning sun for hours in order to pass through the checkpoint and leave Ramallah for work or medical care. Four hundred Women in Black stood at the checkpoint holding anti-occupation signs, while on the Ramallah side of the checkpoint Palestinian women were chanting and trying to cross the checkpoint.

To be sure, the checkpoints work to foreclose the possibility of co-habitation, or, to put it differently, to make the relational form of dispossession impossible. But this condition of bodily enclosure and exposure can become the occasion not only of subjugation but also of resilience, courage, and struggle. So yes, there is a dialectic of presence/absence that goes on in this differentially distributed political condition of bodily exposure, whereby presence (or a presence-effect) is produced by being constantly haunted by its spectral absences or (mis)recognized presences – the inassimilable remains of its ontological horizon. The specter would refer, in this context, to the insistent and insinuating anti-ontological remains, foreclosed and yet surviving, from the normative demarcation of the self-present human. Or, to phrase it yet another way: it is the trace that remains from the other's uncanny presence as absence – her present absence. But let me clarify at this point that my summoning the lexicon of the specter here is not meant to conjure away corporeality. Not at all. In my understanding, the specter involves a return to some sort of bodily presence, be it displaced, dismembered, enclosed, or foreclosed. As Derrida writes at the beginning of his *Specters of Marx*: "For there is no ghost, there is never any becoming specter of the spirit without at least the appearance of flesh, in a space of invisible visibility like the disappearing of an apparition. For the ghost, there must be a return to the body, but to a body that is more abstract than ever."[5] So when I refer to the political conditions of bodily exposure, whereby presence is constantly haunted by its spectral absences, I seek to address what it means and takes for a spectral body to make itself present. I am interested in how hauntology (to recall again Derrida's notion of haunting) might function as a critique of ontology. What possibilities for theory and practice might this shift open? How might we re-imagine performativity through this troubling of conventional categorizations of the ontological?

So I am not sure whether presence can be ever distinguished from, or divested of, the canonical metaphysical guises of self-identity and self-sufficiency once and for all. But it can never be totally subsumed by them either. To articulate this double bind is also, I would argue, to pose the question of radicalizing performativity, and therefore to pose a question that must be left in suspense. Self-identity carries the genealogical burden of a metaphysics of presence, but, at the same time, it is not determined by the burden of the histories in which it has been entrenched. Being dispossessed by the other's presence and by our own presence to the other is the only way to be present to one another. So being present to one another takes place at the limits of one's own self-sufficiency and self-knowability, in the wake of the endless finitude of the human. In order to be present to one another (but also to be absent to, or missed by, another), we are called to take over, and occasionally to give away, the norms through which we are established as selves and others. We are necessarily implicated in the desires and the anxieties of presence and propriation. But we are also capable of expropriating the limitations and injuries prescribed by them. The problem then remains of how to seek out the impossible and yet necessary possibility of being present to one another, "fully there," in ways not assimilated or submitted to the ontological presuppositions of normative authoritarian self-presence.

The logic of appropriation and dispossession, whether it be colonial or neocolonial, capitalist, and neoliberal, endures by reproducing a metaphysics of presence in the form of the violence inherent in improper, expropriated, and dispossessed subjectivities. In fact, dispossession emerges as a crucial force of ontopological modes of preconfigured bodies, subjectivities, communities, identities, truths, and political economies of life. Taking cue from Derrida's notion of "ontopology," which links the ontological value of being to a certain determined *topos*, locality, or territory,[6] we might track the ways in which dispossession carries within it regulatory practices related to the conditions of situatedness, displacement, and emplacement, practices that produce and constrain human intelligibility. This means that the logic of dispossession is interminably mapped onto our bodies, onto particular bodies-in-place, through normative matrices but also through situated practices of raciality, gender, sexuality, intimacy, able-bodiedness, economy, and citizenship. It produces dispossessed subjectivities, rendering them subhuman or hauntingly all-too-human, binding them within calculable self-same identities, and putting them in their proper place – the only spatial condition of being that they can possibly occupy, namely one of perennial occupation as non-being and non-having. So a metaphysics of presence is mapped onto particular bodies, selves, and lives as absence, obliteration, and unarchivable spectrality.

JB: Can you explain more about how you see a subject grounded in the metaphysics of presence dominating, regulating, or constituting those whose proper place is non-being? I am thinking here about "non-being" as it relates, say, to the idea of "social death" (Patterson),[7] or those who are left to die through negligence (Mbembe),[8] or those who live with a higher risk of mortality (Gilmore).[9] I am wondering about how those whose "proper place is non-being" might be described in terms of precarity, or whether that term works in another way.

AA: In designating the politically induced condition in which certain people and groups of people become differentially exposed to injury, violence, poverty, indebtedness, and death, "precarity" describes exactly the lives of those whose "proper place is non-being." This is indeed related to socially assigned disposability (a condition which proves fundamental to the neoliberal regime) as well as to various modalities of valuelessness, such as social death, abandonment, impoverishment, state and individual racism, fascism, homophobia, sexual assault, militarism, malnutrition, industrial accidents, workplace injuries, privatization, and liberal governmentalization of aversion and empathy. Achille

Mbembe's insistence on the link between sovereignty and exposure to death is relevant here. As a global modality of power that subjects populations to conditions that ascribe them the status of living dead, "necropolitics" determines who can be wasted and who cannot; it distinguishes those who are disposable from those who are not; and it does so in both spectacular and quotidian ways, insistently and insinuatingly.[10] In such contexts, the power of dispossession works by rendering certain subjects, communities, or populations unintelligible, by eviscerating for them the conditions of possibility for life and the "human" itself. The violent logic of dispossession seeks to reassert the propriety of both spatiality and subjectivity as it bodies forth displaced and displaceable subjectivities, as it challenges them to take their proper place instead of taking place. But where and how do the lives of those whose "proper place is non-being" take place after the critique of the metaphysics of substance? How is the "substance" of these lives produced?

JB: I appreciate your conception of "assigned disposability," since it highlights this characteristic of neoliberal regimes to allocate disposability and precarity. This is especially important to remember if we want to understand the difference between precarity as an existential category that is presumed to be equally shared, and precarity as a condition of induced inequality and destitution. The latter is a way of exploiting an existential condition, since precarity, understood as a vulnerability to injury and loss, can never be reversed (this I tend to call precariousness), and yet the differential ways of allocating precarity, of assigning disposability, are clearly aims and effects of neoliberal forms of social and economic life.

And yet, I am wondering whether "the human" would be characterized by you as a being who can take place (assume a place, and also, in some sense, "happen"), and whether this mode of happening emerges when – or through those acts by which – a collectivity refuses to stay in a proper place. It seems that for the human to emerge in your terms, the proper must be displaced. But how would that work if we are thinking about those who are territorially dispossessed? They are compelled to leave their proper place, and in those cases, staying in place is precisely an act of resistance.

AA: Of course. This is why I use the "refusal to stay in one's proper place" to signal acts of radical reterritorialization, which might certainly include remaining in specific places. I summon possibilities of being "elsewhere" in order to suggest that subjection is never fixed and final, even though it "takes place" on such localized and territorialized planes as nation-state, workplace, private property, kinship, nuclear family, and self-centered subjectivity. It is arguably impossible to think of "staying in place" or "refusing to move" as an act of resistance without recalling Rosa Parks, the African-American civil rights activist, who, on December 1, 1955, refused to conform to the bus driver's order that she give up her seat for a white passenger. In times of racial segregation, in Montgomery, Alabama, the first four rows of bus seats were reserved for white passengers, while black people were allowed only in "colored" sections, in the rear of the bus. Parks writes, in her autobiography:

People always say that I didn't give up my seat because I was tired, but that isn't true. I was not tired physically, or no more tired than I usually was at the end of a working day. I was not old, although some people have an image of me as being old then. I was forty-two. No, the only tired I was, was tired of giving in.[11]

So, not giving up one's seat, as an act of civil disobedience, is an enactment of refusal to stay in, or to move to, one's assigned proper place. In this sense, staying in place may require some movement, or displacement. It is an act of ascribing a place to oneself within the social. What interests me in this extraordinary moment of defiance is the intertwined bodily and spatial quality of not-giving-up as not-giving-in. The intertwined bodily and territorial forces of dispossession play out in the exposure of bodies-in-place, which can become the occasion of subjugation, surveillance, and interpellation. It can also become the occasion of situated acts of resistance, resilience, and confrontation with the matrices of dispossession, through appropriating the ownership of one's body from these oppressive matrices. Acted upon, and yet acting, bodies-in-place and bodies-out-of-place at once embody and displace the conditions of intelligible embodiment and agency.

But I think that the facile equation of agency with the capacity to move needs to be problematized also from the perspective of disability studies. Such a reductive construal of agency as moving, mobilizing, or standing up privileges mobility and thus reiterates the presumption that agency belongs properly to certain regimes of bodily morphology and recognizability. It is important to ask ourselves: What other possibilities and

articulations of political agency does the conceptualization of agency in such linear, kinetic, and phonocentric
ways work to foreclose?

Those territorially dispossessed of their land refuse to
stay in their assigned "proper place" (that is, in the
place of displacement imposed by imperial sovereignty)
precisely by staying in place, or claiming the right to
stay in place, and demanding their proprietary rights in
land. At the same time, one must be very careful to
critically grasp and problematize liberal multicultural
pretensions which assert "staying in place" as a cultural
essence, or essential ground, of being "properly" native.
Isn't this incitation to the proper (that is, customary,
"traditional," assimilable, and governable) self-identity
of alterity effectively an instance of colonialist epistemic
violence?

JB: Surely colonial violence can work both ways, by
depriving an indigenous population of their land, and
yet restricting the mobility of that population to the very
land they no longer own. Certainly occupied Palestine
is a case in point, but so, too, are any number of refugee
camps that detain and immobilize at the same time as
they dispossess a population. I think you may be referring to the tactic on the part of European metropoles to
claim that North African and Middle Eastern immigrants do not belong to European "land." The idea that
immigrants should "go back to their land" (a refrain
that has been used by racists in the United States against
African-Americans who are told to return to Africa)
suggests allegiance to the notion of the "autochthonous,"
which means belonging to the chthonic, or the earthly
site. As you know, the Chthonic gods were those who

belonged to the earth and defended its powers. But now, throughout Europe, we hear about the autochthonic, referring to European citizens who are precisely not immigrants. The autochthonic are importantly not the same as the indigenous. The effort to return immigrants to their proper "nations" belongs to this nationalist logic. So we have to think about these two different tactics, and how they work together: restricting a population to a land of which they have been dispossessed and refusing the entry into the European metropole of those who are presumed to belong to another land. One can see how these two modalities of colonial power work together to produce the situation in which the targeted population belongs, finally, to no land, a situation that embodies one clear impasse of dispossession.

AA: Your point about the idea of the "autochthonous" is very important. We should refuse the idea that claiming the right to "stay put" is about "traditional" stasis. As the right-to-the-city movements show, claiming a place is not merely about gaining access to what already exists but rather about transforming place. We could, and we should, also consider here the social movements of displaced and landless farmers (El Movimiento Sin Tierra – the Landless Peasant Movement) and the struggles of indigenous people against water privatization in Bolivia; the struggles for recuperation of land rights and against the multinational oil companies' devastation of indigenous lands in Ecuador; or the protests of the Ogoni and other people of Niger Delta against the destruction of their lands by oil companies.

Political resistance to the violence of dispossession in colonial settler regimes such as Australia and Canada can also be viewed productively through the prism of colonially embedded notions of belonging and unbelonging. Australian Indigenous people's experience and sense of place and belonging are bound up with the dispossession of the land and the denial of indigenous rights. Indigenous people's uprooting, removal to reserves and spatial containment, forced adoptions, and placement in institutions were all enabled and justified by the discursive formation that imagined Australia as an uninhabited land prior to the original dispossession, the notion that it belonged to no one before the invasion of white British settlers in 1788. The juridical doctrine of Terra Nullius (no man's land, wasteland) rendered Indigenous people strangers and homeless, neither belonging nor owning.[12] This wasteland rationale is deployed also as a technique of land appropriation and occupation in the colonial settler context of Palestine, where the Minister of Agriculture is empowered to take over lands not being cultivated, including those of displaced Palestinians.[13]

JB: Yes, but let us remember that land confiscation happens there all the time, whether or not entitled by specific provisions in the law. In fact, the distinction between legal and illegal land confiscation is finally not a very important one, since the legal means are as unjust and illegitimate as the illegal ones.[14] When Netanyahu refers to the settlements in the West Bank as evidence of a "land dispute," he imagines two parties, equal in power, who are submitting their conflicting claims to some neutral arbiter. But Israel is at once the colonial occupier, the maker and arbiter of the rule of law, which means that the rule of law is implicated in the colonial project itself. So though there are on occasion "good decisions" that emerge from Israeli courts, the scene is still one of extraordinary inequality. It is also why efforts at co-existence that do not fundamentally challenge the colonial structure end up ratifying and extending that structure, even offering an alibi for colonialism's "humane" versions.

AA: Yes. Ongoing (post)colonial subjection and dispossession are further legitimated, normalized, and regulated through, and in the name of, discourses of reconciliation, which work to represent Indigenous peoples as silent sufferers.[15] So dispossession, as a way of separating people from means of survival, is not only a problem of land deprivation but also a problem of subjective and epistemic violence; or, put another way, a problem of discursive and affective appropriation, with crucially gendered and sexualized implications. This appropriation of corporeal and affective spaces, which is imbricated with the social construction of victimhood, is a critical aspect of (post)colonial dispossession and its mechanisms of normalization. Veena Das's analysis of the ways in which the discourse of suffering was deployed as a legitimating trope which worked to reduce the suffering of victims to silence and passivity in the aftermath of the Bhopal disaster in India provides an illuminating example of this representational economy of dispossession, domination, victimhood, and alienation.[16]

In order to gain access to the genealogy of the proper(tied) subject, we have to turn to the structure of dispossession that organizes contemporaneous forms of colonialism, slavery, racial and gender violence.[17] In

European colonies, property ownership was a prerequisite for proper political subjectivity and citizenship, but
was also, at the same time, attached to race and gender
requirements – that is, whiteness and maleness – that
signified proper (and propertied) civilized human
subjectivity.[18] Subjectifying and simultaneously desubjectifying and dispossessing violence (as in the genealogies of colonialism and the slave trade, but also the new
imperialism and the neoliberal international order, and
their gendered implications) emerged as a prerequisite
for (property-owning, white, male) subjectivity; such a
subjectivity is constituted through, and inhabited by,
processes of desubjectifying others, rendering them us-
able, employable, but then eventually into waste matter,
or of no use: always available, always expendable. Processes of disposability – as well as the spectral traces of
endurance, the struggles against it, and the political
potentialities emerging within it – lie at the heart of
ongoing colonially and postcolonially embedded notions
of the self-contained, proper(tied), liberal subject.[19]

So a question that arises here, regarding the epistemic
violence inherent in matrices of dispossession and disposability, could be articulated thus: How might claims
for the recognition of rights to land and resources, necessarily inscribed as they are in colonially embedded
epistemologies of sovereignty, territory, and property
ownership, simultaneously work to decolonize the apparatus of property and to unsettle the colonial conceit of
proper and propertied human subjectivity?[20] The challenge is to advance new idioms for contemporary critical
agency by radically questioning the persistent racialized
and sexualized onto-epistemologies of self-contained
and property-owning subjectivity. In the background of

this problematic lie certain questions related to critical thought and agonistic politics: How are normative notions of humanity (and non-human animality) inscribed in attempts at restoring subjects to humanity, and how are they re-inscribed and troubled? What is at stake in employing epistemic regimes of ontologization in our critical discourses in order to question late liberal processes of desubjectivation and exhaustion?

JB: I take it we agree that we have to think about dispossession as one way that subjects are radically de-instituted, as a mode of subjugation that has to be opposed. At the same time, it seems we are both wondering whether "possession" is the name of the counter-movement. Surely reclaiming stolen lands is crucial for many indigenous people's movements, and yet that is something different from defining the subject as one who possesses itself and its object world, and whose relations with others are defined by possession and its instrumentalities. The movement to reclaim land is one that involves people working together, recognizing a common mode of subjugation, and disputing forms of individualism that would produce "exceptions" and "heroes." So if a certain kind of political mobilization, even one against land dispossession, is based on an idea of social interdependency, or on modes of ownership that sometimes seek recourse to sovereignty (as the political movements in Hawaii do), this suggests that land reclamations work with and against traditional notions of sovereignty.

AA: I would add that this understanding of the crucial ways in which dispossession inhabits the vicissitudes

and critical possibilities of subjectivation, desubjectivation, and dehumanization offers a useful insight into
how dispossession persists beyond the colony and the
postcolony. In the context of neoliberal forms of capital
– combined with tightened migration policies and the
abjection of stateless people, *sans papiers*, "illegal"
immigrants – bodies (that is, human capital) are becoming increasingly disposable, dispossessed by capital and
its exploitative excess, uncountable and unaccounted
for. At the same time they are individuated and subjec-
tivated through subtler and reflexive biopolitical techniques of self-formation, self-care, self-fashioning, and
self-governance.[21] To be sure, these techniques of power,
just like resources and vulnerability, are differently and
unevenly distributed among different bodies – differently racialized and gendered bodies. Under the auspices
of neoliberal governance, the global biopolitical administration of life and death is reinvented, revitalized, and
reconfigured. This is evidenced in the war on terror,
economic disparities and exhaustion, the normalization
of poverty and precarity in contexts of capitalist crisis-
management, racism, policing of migration, and ongoing
regimes of colonial occupation.

Nonetheless, let me offer a caveat regarding the ways
in which neoliberal governmentality invests in the matter
of the human. I don't think it would be accurate to
argue that what shapes our particular neoliberal phase
is an "anachronistic" configuration of power centered
on death rather than life. Contemporary forms of liberal
governance have not been merely regressing to earlier,
negative, non-humanistic, and injurious forces. Nor
should we invoke the repressive hypothesis in order to
challenge late liberalism and its excesses. Rather than

narratives of periodization marked by the reductive logic of progress and regress, I would suggest that we work once again toward a non-linear critique of contemporary formations of power and modes of constitution of subjectivities that accounts for the contemporaneous and inseparable manifestations of desubjectivation and subjectivation, dehumanization and humanization: "letting live" and "making die," "making live" and "letting die," to use Foucault's rhetorical terms of analysis of state racism in *Society Must Be Defended*.[22] Against a reductive reading of Foucault's genealogy of biopolitics, which tends to bracket or downplay one modality of power in favor of another (for example, "positive" versus "negative"), we need to account for and critically engage the integral co-implication and coevalness of "repressive" and "productive" formations of governing the self and others. To be sure, liberal colonial power has depended on the constitution of subjectivities and affective attachments. We know this from numerous critical thinkers, from Fanon to Ann Stoler; the latter has insightfully traced the critical role played by structures of intimacy in creating racialized and sexualized categories of imperial governance in late nineteenth- and early twentieth-century Indonesia.[23] And contemporary neoliberal power, in all its repressive, subjugating, brutal, and thanatopolitical force of profit extraction, has not lost its performative bio-productivity in capacitating modes of living subjectivity as well as in inculcating normative fantasies and truth-effects of the "good life"[24] in self-owned subjects (a life defined, for instance, by property ownership, commodity fetishism, consumer excitement, securitarian regimes, national belonging, bourgeois self-fashioning,

and biopolitical normalcy). Rather, neoliberal governmentality of the present moment invests – politically,
psychically, and economically – in the production and
management of forms of life: it "makes live," in inculcating modes of one's fashioning of one's "own" life,
while shattering and economically depleting certain live-
lihoods, foreclosing them, rendering them disposable
and perishable. This politico-affective dynamic of (de)
subjectivation through constantly producing, governing, and thwarting aspirations seems to be foundational
to late liberal "economies of abandonment," to invoke
Elizabeth Povinelli's term.[25] In this view it might be
useful to raise, again and again, the question what such
critical exercise would mean for apprehending the political in our political present of (neo)liberal governmental
technologies of the self. What would such engagement
with today's reconfigurations of biopolitical governance
mean for progressive critical thought and politics in
late liberalism, in the wake of anti-colonial and anti-
capitalist movements? What could the present become
from the scene of the performative politics of survival
and alternative forms of life?

Such racialized and sexualized colonially inscribed
forms of power involved in the property–propriety
economies of the modern subject and place produce
incommensurate onto-epistemologies of humanness and
non-humanness, possession and dispossession, livability
and unlivability. When it comes to "the human," the
matter that must be addressed constantly and forcefully
is the differential allocation of humanness: the perpetually shifting and variably positioned boundary between
those who are rendered properly human and those who
are not, those who are entitled to a long life and those

relegated to slow death. The human cannot be presumed, then. The point here is not to introduce a distinction or temporal spacing between a pre-existing, original and inherent humanness which only later comes to take form through being variably allocated under contingent power configurations. Rather, the point is that the human has no "proper" place to take outside social situatedness and allocation, including the exposure to the possibility of being undone. The human is always the event of its multiple exposures – both within its relatedness to others and within its exposure to the normative forces that arrange the social, political, and cultural matrices of humanness. The eventness of the human includes also gestures that displace the proper of the human, that is, its presumed self-evidence as a predicate to a man with property and propriety. Such gestures motivate questions such as: To whom does the human belong, or who owns the human? Who or what holds the place of the human? Whose humanity is dispossessed? What are the ellipses through which the human takes place? What kind of human is constituted as inhuman or less than human? These are questions that expose the ways in which "the human" has historically become a default mechanism for upholding the intersecting matrices of colonial expansion, phallocentrism, heteronormativity, and possessive individualism. They are, at the same time, questions that, inadvertently or not, and inevitably or not, reiterate the link between the human and ownership. (To whom does the human *belong*? And who *owns* the human?)

So, reckoning the human involves addressing the norms by which intelligibility as human is conferred: an intelligibility without which the human must remain out of place, on the far side of being and becoming. At the same time, the univocal category of the human is perpetually troubled and haunted by the quivering humanity of those living, differing, sexing, mattering, touched and touching otherwise, elsewhere.

JB: You mean to say that any version of the "human" is haunted by a disavowed loss, and no version of the human can fully overcome this disavowal?

AA: Yes. This does not imply, however, a call to broaden the coercive monologism of "the human" by including its previously excluded or dis-appropriated surplus, but rather a challenge to the normative terms by which the human is established through producing disavowed losses and avowed excesses. Although they are normatively represented in terms of taxonomic exteriority, such losses and excesses are fundamentally internal to the authoritative abstraction of the human in functioning as its condition of possibility. They assume either the form of discursive production of the inhuman or the form of discursive ellipsis from representable, imaginable, and recognizable humanness. I am thinking, for example, of Adorno's conception of the inhuman as necessary for the human.[26] In either case, the violation of a life that has been discursively figured as inhuman, or that has been omitted from human discursivity, or that has been conditionally included as an uncannily authentic human, is not perceived as violation. Address and redress of this violence cannot find a place in the world as it is. In this sense, if "the human" can ever take place (assume a place, but also "happen") in terms of radical and subversive resignification, this taking place might happen through the human refusing to stay in its proper place. Thus the "ontopology" of the human has a bearing on the question of mattering, that is, on the question of the differential (de)constitution and (de) valuation of human matter and humans that matter. So rather than a rehabilitation of the humanist subject in the form of liberal tolerance or assimilatory inclusion of ready-made identities, the political potential of this critique, if there is any, would be to subvert those norms and open the human to radical rearticulations of humanness.

JB: I am following you here, but I am hesitating. Is there not a tension between an avowed excess and a disa-vowed loss (the mark of melancholy)? Are these two different ways of describing what gets placed or pro-duced outside the boundary of the human something that then "exceeds" its boundaries and so installs and maintains those boundaries from the outside? Are we talking about a loss that cannot be avowed, or are we talking about an excess that is itself a radicalization of the experience of loss, one that becomes a form of avowal, if not a labor of avowal? Is this what happens, for instance, when the barbarian, the monster, or the animal takes to the street?

I follow you in adding the animal to our discussions for several reasons: it seems to me that the animal has the status of being both inside and outside the human form; it also seems that there is a street politics for the animal (consider the fate of street cats in Rome); finally, to pursue these questions it appears that we have to struggle against those versions of the human that assume the animal as its opposite, and to instead propose a claim for human animality. This last seems very important not only in order to rethink the materialist basis of the human, but also because we cannot understand human life without understanding that its modes are connected up with other forms of life by which it is distinguished and with which it is continuous. If we are moving toward a relational view, then it would follow that the human not only has a relation to animals (conceived as the other), but is itself implicated in its own animality. That animality is its own and not yet its own, which is why both animality and life constitute and exceed whatever we call the human. The point is not to find the right typology, but to understand where typological thinking falls apart. The human animal might be one way of naming that collapse of typological distinction.

I would agree as well that as much as we are trying to criticize the "proper" of the "properly human," we are also trying to know in what way the loss of what is properly one's own is crucial for any understanding of misappropriation (of land, of goods, of labor), or even of stealing and expulsion. The challenge of the proper shows, in part, that the human and the animal are linked, and that other forms of linkage and connection are part of any mobilization against political and economic dispossession. So we have to continue to ask about that profound pull or temptation to counter the dispossession of human beings with more robust ideas of human possession. When we treat the problem as if it were a simple dialectical reversal, we cannot ask another set of questions: Who and what is excluded from the "human," and how has the category of the "human" come to be formed against the background of the abject or the disavowed?[27] In other words, how has the human been formed and maintained on the condition of a set of dispossessions?

AA: I take your point about the tension between a disavowed loss and an avowed excess. I would just say, in a very sketchy way, that if the former refers to that which gets abjected or foreclosed from the human, the latter denotes forms of life that are conferred recognition as human according to the established norms of recognizability, on the condition of and at the cost of conforming to these norms. If disavowed loss refers to what gets placed outside the boundary of the human, avowed excess might be taken to describe what is produced in a way of exclusionary inclusion; such beings remain superfluous, in a way, and yet they get slyly and conditionally interpellated in the all-too-intelligible categories of the normative human. But, of course, these occasions do not refer to a fixed, ontological distinction. What gets produced outside the boundary of the human can "exceed" its boundaries and so maintain or trouble those boundaries from the outside.

It seems to me that what links these two occasions – in a relation of tension, certainly – is the radical potential that emerges from the losses, repudiations, foreclosures, and normative acknowledgements through which human intelligibility is constituted. So yes, a radicalization of the experience of loss would expose or challenge those regulative fictions that produce the unintelligible, albeit not in totalizing and teleological ways. As you put it, "Is this what happens, for instance, when the barbarian, the monster, or the animal takes to the street?" We could add: the stranger, the *sans papiers*, the unemployed, the queer. As we struggle today, jointly and partially, in present circumstances when matters of survival are at stake, queerness, anti-racism, anti-precarity, and companion-species solidarity really matter as enactments of struggles and transformative modes of survival. In bringing up the animal and the monster, you aptly add relationality to our perspective on the human form. In order to pursue this question, we have to rethink the materiality of the human through amalgamations and reassemblages of the animate and inanimate, human and non-human, animal and human animal, life and death. Being invariably in communities with other forms of life, in social realms of co-implicated and differently embodied bodies, serves in the first place as an unsettling of the fantasy of a self-sufficient human subject; it also offers a necessary means for comprehending being-in-common, beyond communitarianism and anthropomorphism, as a condition of new possibilities for politics – a politics that involves engaging with the biopolitical condition while also revisiting the humanist premises of the (bio)political.

3
A caveat about the
"primacy of economy"

AA: As we speak about the radical possibility and necessity of disrupting the terms that define the political in our times, let me unravel a concern and invite your response. As we revisit the political, ethical, and affective economies of dispossession, I would like to say that I am perplexed about a particular political and theoretical tendency to privilege and reify the category of the "economy" in light of the current financial crisis. Of course this tendency has been circulating for some time, along with its concomitant discourses of the division between "primary" and "secondary" conditions of oppression, whereby the former is represented by the "material" and the "economic" while the latter by the "merely cultural."[1] Circulating among progressive intellectuals during the 1980s was an objection to the purported abandonment of the materialist project. It was the moment at which poststructuralism was demonized as politically paralyzing. I worry that at the present moment in left intellectual and political history that discourse might regain a currency, as neoliberalism compels us all to a renewed acknowledgement and affirmation of the so-called primacy of economy. The current moment might be portrayed as a new and reinvigorated incitation to economic discourse, which comes in various forms (very heterogeneous otherwise): either as post-political technocratic therapeutics and financial management, or as critical, anti-capitalist, and anti-neoliberal visions that take the economic realm to offer the only possible arena in which a comprehensive and rigorous political position against neoliberalism might be wrought. If I am right in the depiction I venture here, this resumption of economistic orthodoxy works epistemologically in tandem with neoliberal logic. Would this re-packaging of the economy's primacy harbinger a resurgent social conservatism on the Left? I hasten to add, however, that there are certainly several left movements and collectivities in the world today that are aware of such predicaments and respond successfully to such challenges.

I have no doubt that "economy" is today a diffuse, insidious, and powerful interpellation through which subjects (and non-subjects) are called into formation and reformulation. But I would argue that the current historical moment is not merely about the economy *itself* (if such a thing exists), and, even more significantly, economy is not merely about the economic "itself." Perhaps one might reformulate this caveat thus: there is nothing merely economic about economics.

JB: So you are suggesting that rendering the economic domain autonomous is a way of accepting the claims of economic science and calculation proffered by neoliberalism? I believe this follows upon an older point made by Marx – and Marxist economic anthropologists – that one of the achievements of capitalism was the analytic distinction between the domain of the social and the domain of the economic. "Disembedding" economic structures from their social and historical conditions and conventions is precisely the condition of economic formalism.

AA: This is exactly my point, but allow me to be more specific. The current regimes of power prompt pressing and complicated questions about how to think and how to act in order to counter these regimes as well as about how to engage with the materialities of life that are being produced through them. Unsettling the hegemony of capitalism involves opening up conceptual, discursive, affective, and political spaces for enlarging our economic and political imaginary. It requires exploring also what circulating forms and norms of surplus appropriation the formalistic preoccupation with neoliberal economics works to obscure. I think it is critical that we pay close attention to the ways in which neoliberalism is not just a mode of economic management and corporate governance, but rather, and even more significantly, a "political rationality" (in concurrence with Wendy Brown[2]), or a matrix of intelligibility that works to replace the political with technocratic, corporate, post-political governance. The production of dispensable and disposable populations (echoing the "surplus population" in Marx's formulation) has everything to do with questions of racism, sexism, homophobia, heteronormativity, ableism, and familialism, all those questions that have been historically discounted as irrelevant to "real" politics. The capitalism of our times has everything to do with the biopolitics of social Darwinism — with all its implications of race, gender, sexuality, class, and ability – inherent in neoliberal governmentality. My sense is that the biopolitical is at the heart of the logics, fantasies, and technologies that engender the political and moral economies of our late liberal times.

JB: But perhaps there are two different points here. The first is about the construction of an autonomous economic system, one whose workings require formal models that delimit and separate off economic processes from other social and historical ones. The second seems to be an argument with a form of Marxism that continues to argue for, or to presume uncritically, primary and secondary forms of oppression. How do we think the "extra-economic" within the economic in response to the first problem? And how do we refuse the dismissal of the "merely cultural" implied by the second? I gather what you are also saying is that some left criticisms end up reproducing the presumption of autonomy of the economic sphere, as well as its primacy in the determination of social and political reality. It seems, too, that you are suggesting that understanding neoliberalism as a *political rationality* (cf. Wendy Brown) is one way to cut across the economic/cultural divide and dispense with the model of primary and secondary determinations and its economistic reductions.

AA: Exactly. Of course, the concepts and epistemologies that we deploy in order to deconstruct the current orders of power are necessarily implicated in these orders, ones that divide the world into separate spheres (economy, society, culture, politics) and are invested in the production of a distinctive economic sphere. But I think we need to imagine and enact alternative (that is, non-economistic) ways to deploy the concept of "economy" beyond its common sense. It becomes necessary once again to raise the questions: Does capitalism, in its current neoliberal mutation as state of exception (that is, "crisis"), inevitably interpellate us today as subjects of economy and subjects of competitive economic struggle for survival? Does it also recruit us into an ideological framework that affirms the anachronistic division between the "material" and the "cultural"? How do we resist and fight neoliberal log(ist)ics without reducing our politics to an economistic politics? Are we perhaps running the risk of letting ongoing political contestation be colonized by a purportedly distinct economic configuration that masquerades as the only really serious and robust arena of politics? I think that one of the formative effects of this incitation to economic reductionism is the dismissal of apparently non-economistic, or uneconomic, perspectives as being preoccupied with secondary, derivative, particularistic, inessential, and, "in the final analysis," *trivial* matters and forms of politics. So it is relevant to consider and offer non-economistic and uneconomic perspectives on contemporary politics. It seems to me that the challenge today is to better understand how the normativity of the economic in its neoliberal guise is inevitably and fundamentally linked to the reproduction of gender, sexual, kinship, desire, and biopolitical (that is, bio-capital, human capital) normativity.

A *caveat* about the *"primacy of economy"*

JB: In a sense, we are confronted again with the challenge taken up by socialist feminisms a few decades ago, and one that continues to be important to those who are thinking about the economy of the household, the reproduction of labor, the differential production of illiteracy and poverty. One reason I am interested in precarity, which would include a consideration of "precaritization," is that it describes that process of acclimatizing a population to insecurity. It operates to expose a targeted demographic to unemployment or to radically unpredictable swings between employment and unemployment, producing poverty and insecurity about an economic future, but also interpellating that population as expendable, if not fully abandoned. These affective registers of precaritization include the lived feeling of precariousness, which can be articulated with a damaged sense of future and a heightened sense of anxiety about issues like illness and mortality (especially when there is no health insurance or when conditions of labor and accelerated anxiety converge to debilitate the body). This is just one example of how a condition crosses the economic and cultural spheres, suggesting that what we need precisely are a new set of transversal categories and forms of thought that elude both dualism and determinism.

4

Sexual dispossessions

AA: In the context of poststructuralist and psychoanalytic feminist theorizations of gender and sexuality, dispossession might be connected to a crucial constitutive and regulatory fiction of gender and sexuality – namely having versus not having. Having versus not having the phallus, in its inextricable relation with the distinction between *being* and *having* the phallus, lies at the heart of presumptions of materiality that construct truth regimes of sex, gender, and the body.

JB: I am wondering if we can think together about what happens when we put "constitutive" together with "regulatory fiction." Do we mean to say that a certain fiction regulates the formation of gender as well as sexuality? Regulation and constitution are often thought as separate sorts of activities, so to put them together suggests that the means through which gender and sexuality are regulated are also the condition of possibility for their emergence. In other words, regulatory ideals give shape and trajectory to emergent gender and sexuality. Does this dual operation of power function in the same way for gender as for sexuality? It seems to me that it might be important to separate the regulatory constitution of gender from the regulatory constitution of sexuality, and that we cannot assume enduring structural or causal links between the two. Admittedly, they are very often implicated in one another, but to understand how, we need to have a situational analysis. I would not want to say that the regulation of gender is only or always in the service of regulating sexuality, or that the regulation of sexuality has as its primary aim the stabilization of gender norms. That can sometimes be true, but it is surely as often the case that these two regulatory modes work at cross-purposes or in ways that prove to be relatively indifferent to one another.

AA: In response to your very important question about what it means to put together "constitutive" and "regulatory" modes of power, I would say that this gesture of bringing-together perhaps seeks to invoke the ambivalent and provisional powers of subjectivation, which both constitute subjects and regulate them, as you say, but in various and contingent ways, intensities, contexts, and dispersals, and in ways that encompass – albeit not seamlessly actualize and control – the subjects' erotic attachments to the identity designations they are called to assume and perform. What is important in the scene of subjectivation is that desire and the law are inextricably intertwined. In this performative intertwinement, gender and sexual categories, identities, and fantasies are reconstituted and reinvented in unforeseen ways as the law "strives" (such a depiction of power as intentional and teleological is only catachrestic here) to produce, affirm, consolidate, thwart, commodify, or render them proper. Perhaps it would be critical to reflect on the ways in which "constitutive" and "regulatory," as well as the relation between them, get fabricated, reshaped, rewoven, and reassembled in this provisional and contestable process. So my sense is that the disruption of the conceptual transition between constitution and regulation is a way to suggest, as you say, that the means through which gender and sexuality are regulated can be also the condition of possibility for their emergence. It is true that this formulation leaves us with a battery of questions. I wonder, for example, whether the difficulty with pondering this link between constitution and regulation might have to do with the presumed distinction between primary and secondary moments in the process of subjectivation (that is, "primary narcissism" and "secondary narcissism"). How can we comprehend the incitation to perform and conform beyond this perspective of chronological transition, which makes us assume a *pre*-discursive body and a *primary* intention of power as transitive and external to this body? In order to do that, we might need to deconstruct the epistemological division between a primary, productive and affirmative, power as constitutive of the subject and a secondary, regulatory or subordinating, power as external to that subject. We will also need to destabilize both a certain ontological perspective of power, whereby power is akin to a property that can be possessed or alienated, and concomitant accounts of subjectivity, whereby the subject is regarded as a self-possessed and possessive agent. And so this discussion takes us to the inherently ambivalent and undecidable forces of subjectivation in both its constitutive and regulatory workings and beyond the problematic discrimination between "positive" and "negative" aspects of power. Instead of distinguishing "productive" from "destructive" modes of power, then, we might seek to conceptualize the productive destructiveness and the destructive productiveness inherent in our contemporary biopolitical moment.

JB: Well, I do not know whether there is a single "biopolitical moment" right now, or whether there is a field of the biopolitical that operates very differently depending on what place we have in mind. I think there are some ambivalences of this kind that we can easily see within the fields of gay and lesbian rights and human rights in particular. I remember being told years ago that in public I had to say that homosexuality is not a choice. In fact, I think the issue of "choice" is very complicated when it comes to what we call "sexual orientation." Indeed, I've been convinced by Leticia Sabsay that there is also something very problematic about the idea of "sexual orientation," given that it ascribes a disposition to a subject, and so provides a radically arelational account of sexuality.[1] A mode of sexuality and its "object choice" can be recurrent, even obsessively so, but does that necessarily qualify that mode of sexual discernment as an "orientation"? When and how (and why?) do we seek to distinguish so rigorously between act, practice, and identity? The reason that sexual orientation was supposed to remain "unchosen" is that it could qualify as an involuntary social characteristic, and so would deserve special protection against discrimination under the law. Is sexual orientation analogous to "disability" or to "political belief"?[2] I am not sure; might it necessarily span connections between the two? Although I support legal struggles against discrimination on the basis of sexuality, I wonder what happens when we take the idea of "sexual orientation" for granted within ordinary discourse.

Similarly, the human rights discourse that establishes sexuality as a kind of right that is borne by a subject, or that should be so borne, is one that appeals to notions of "free expression" as well as to very culturally specific ideas of what free expression is. The definition that seeks to protect the rights of those who are not free to express their sexuality ends up establishing an ideal, if not a norm, of what the free expression of sexuality should look like. The prescription of certain cultural ideas of "freedom" that involve hyper-visibility and discourses of "outness" thus becomes a way of exporting and imposing certain first-world conceptions of freedom's contours. Even if we accept that there are visible and audible domains of freedom, this should ideally provide a point of departure for asking about cultural practices of sexuality and of sexual freedom that do not conform to that one view. Joseph Massad's criticism of the gay international in *Desiring Arabs*[3] is one such example of this. As we can see, sometimes the norms that are supposed to "set us free" end up operating as constraints on the very freedom they are meant to protect. At such moments, we have to wonder what forms of cultural narrowness keep us from asking how norms that sometimes function in the name of freedom can also become vehicles of cultural imperialism and unfreedom. We have seen such reversals of function in the idea that the United States waged war in Afghanistan to liberate its women ("liberation" becomes another name for what licenses bombing), as well as the idea that Israel is impressively democratic, a bastion of human rights, because of the intensification of gay capital in Tel Aviv (where "the outness" of gay life serves as an instrument to deflect from the oppression of Palestinians under occupation, Palestinians with damaged citizenship within Israel, and those in forced exile, wagering on a nefarious assumption that Palestine is coextensive with homophobia).

AA: This is clearly connected with the issue of growing homonationalism within global queer organizing.[4] In contexts of migration management, for example, the liberal state legislates in ways that incorporate feminist and queer subjectivities into the mainstream fold of the nation-state. I too find very powerful Leticia Sabsay's claim that there is something extremely problematic about the idea of "sexual orientation," given that it works to ascribe a disposition to subjects, and so to reproduce an arelational account of sexuality. I think we need to break with the impossible dilemma: chosen versus unchosen, or voluntary "political belief" versus involuntary "disability." On the contrary, we need to trace how configurations of sex/gender/sexuality get incorporated into the liberal politics and the biopolitical agendas of the nation-state and how they might work to unsettle and oppose them.

But let's try to ponder how sex/gender/sexuality conjunctures might be implicated in the matrices and processes of dispossession. In the context of the phallic ideal and the heterosexual matrix, having versus not having the phallus renders the phallus as an invariably proper, fixed, and inalienable possession of male anatomy. This inalienable and self-controlling possessiveness posits the regulatory fiction of an originating and pre-discursive materiality. This is, however, an area both persistent and contested. As you have unraveled these threads in *Bodies That Matter*, the phallus is rendered transferable and expropriable through its very idealization as a privileged trope of masculine morphology; it can only be approximated, not possessed. It comes to signify through a tenuous, deterritorialized, and transient spectralization, rather than through a structural place of originary possessiveness vis-à-vis the boundaries of sex. As it is transfigured through different body parts, body-like things and accessories, or bodily performances, both recalling and displacing the masculine phallic ideal, the whole signifying schema of "having" is dispossessed from its place as a hegemonic imaginary and an essential figure of power. It is the phallus's incapacity to establish the morphological unity and territorial stability it names that enables provisional critical mimeses that traverse and transfigure the "masculine"–"feminine" binarism. The deconstruction of normative "having," however, does not necessarily entail the essentialist gesture of inventing a "new having." As you put it in *Bodies That Matter*: "[W]hat is needed is not a new body part, as it were, but a displacement of the hegemonic symbolic of (heterosexist) sexual difference and the critical release of alternative imaginary schemas for constituting sites of erotogenic pleasure."[5] So critical mimesis is not about establishing a new foundational materiality as a matter of identitarian definition; it is, rather, a contingent occasion of subversive repetition redeploying the malleability of the norm and the fictive character of its naturalization.

Perhaps this formulation allows us to shift the way sexual categorization is normatively framed through the presumptions of authentic and authoritative possession. Contingent, mutable, imitative, and critically dispossessed bodily morphologies, falling outside their normative taken-for-grantedness, give us a way of imagining sexed bodies not through a sexual categorization predicated upon inherent properties, but rather through the possibilities of imitative performative practices without an original. But I guess I would be interested in hearing you reflect upon some of your work on sexuality here. I would like to hear how you read (or how you would rewrite) all of this today.

JB: It is interesting to read this description. I am sure it is a good description that includes some of my views from *Bodies That Matter*. I am asking myself as I read your remarks whether I still hold to these views. Indeed, who was this person who held these views? I see that to a certain extent you hold them, or you hold them out to me, and I appreciate the way you give back, but I am less certain now than before whether I want this gift! It is true that the alternative of "having" and "being" that structures the Lacanian phallus discourse raises the question of property, or of having property in one's body, of regarding various "parts" as one's property. But it may be that to "have" the phallus is to be *the one* who has the phallus rather than the one who must be the phallus for that one. In that case, the phallus is not a property that anyone can have outside of an imaginary relation. There has to be another, perhaps a "you" before whom anyone can "have" the phallus. If no one is the phallus, then no one has it. This means that the relation between acquisition and having is a fragile one. And if Lacan is right, and "there is no sexual relation," then the being and the having function in different, even incommensurable, modalities – which is why the non-existing sexual relation is also a comedy. They require one another, but they are in some way mismatched, permanently. Like many other feminists in the 1980s and '90s, I wondered whether the penis is the anatomical ground and prerogative for "having" the phallus. The Lacanians mainly respond by saying that the "having" belongs to an order that does not depend upon the anatomical. And yet how are we to understand this order? We can, for instance, see that certain gendered interpretive schemas function throughout the history of science to determine anatomical differences, and that these have changed over time. The very determination of anatomical parts takes place through an interpretive scheme. The debates about how to determine sex, how to establish, for instance, an intersexual condition, depend on how one draws the line around the organ. Indeed, it seems to me that there is no organ without the delimitation of the organ. That does not mean that the delimitation brings the sexual organ into being. It means only that any sexual organ that is recognized as such has passed through a perceptual process of delimitation or demarcation. Since any delimitation follows from a practice of delimitation that is itself the result of a history of such practices, it seems to follow that our sexual organs are saturated with historical interpretations, even before we discover them and start what Freud called infantile theoretical investigations.

The discourse of organs, though, has also passed through "organ donation" and "organ markets" and, even more pertinently, organ removal and enhancement. Transsexuals seeking operations focus on the removal of the organ or its construction, as do women who seek breast enlargement or reduction. We can think of many other instances in which serious and urgent desires for morphological change are negotiated in the language of medical markets. I reject the notion that medical technology unilaterally produces such desires, just as I reject the notion that individuals choose such alterations from conscious considerations alone. There are powerful desires and histories that act upon us as we seek to craft a history of desire for ourselves, to emerge in bodily forms partially given and partially crafted. Acted upon, yet acting, the "we" who we are is caught always precisely there, at the nexus of temporal demands from the past and the future.

It is important to consider what it might mean to conceive of erotic "togetherness" "released from" heteronormativity. It is important to hold out for that possibility, and to realize that no matter how hegemonic heteronormativity may be (and it does take many forms, no?), it also fails to work as well as it might appear. After all, one finds queerness piercing through the heterosexual norm as much as one finds it thriving outside the norm – so it is important not to posit an airtight and totalizing system. (I understand this to be an important critical point offered in the work of Eve Kosofsky Sedgwick when she warned us against paranoid theory.[6]) So I find myself wondering about the emancipatory language of "release": surely, there is some release, the release of possibility, the release of pleasure. But release always struggles with and against forces of recuperation and domestication, so does it follow upon subjection, as liberation follows oppression? I am not sure. It seems to me that sexuality is always returning to the binds from which it seeks release, and so perhaps follows a different kind of rhythm and temporality than most emancipatory schemes would suggest.

5

(Trans)possessions, or bodies beyond themselves

AA: In tracing the possibility of de-privileging or recon-figuring the normative apparatus of "having versus not having" in gender and sexuality, we get at a central aporia of body politics: we lay claim to our bodies as our own, even as we recognize that we cannot ever own our bodies. Our bodies are beyond themselves. Through our bodies we are implicated in thick and intense social processes of relatedness and interdepend-ence; we are exposed, dismembered, given over to others, and undone by the norms that regulate desire, sexual alliance, kinship relations, and conditions of humanness. We are dispossessed by others, moved toward others and by others, affected by others and able to affect others. We are dispossessed by norms, prohibi-tions, self-policing guilt, and shame, but also by love and desire. At the same time, we are dispossessed by normative powers that arrange the uneven distribution of freedoms: territorial displacement, evisceration of means of livelihood, racism, poverty, misogyny, homo-phobia, military violence.

Thus, one of our many dispossessions is by the norms of sex and gender, which precede and exceed our reach, despite the normalizing claims to original and stable proprietary bodily schemas. When I articulate *my* gender or *my* sexuality, when I pronounce the gender or the sexuality that I *have*, I inscribe myself in a matrix of dispossession, expropriability, and relational affectability. But this idea that we own our gender, in an inalienable and unambiguous way, is historically and culturally specific. It is worth considering, for example, Marilyn Strathern's insights into Melanesian gender, whereby gender is figured as transactional and mutable, but also Henrietta Moore's work as well as other anthropological accounts that have relativized western ideas of gender as forms of property.[1]

Transgender suspends the certainties of having versus not having upon which the classic dialectics of recognition is premised in the realms of desire and kinship. Anxiety around the proper object of affectivity and desire plays a crucial role in positioning and depositioning selves in western culture. This normalizing anxiety occasionally fails to sustain itself, however. Consider, for instance, the ways in which the film *Strella* (*A Woman's Way*) (dir. Panos Koutras, Greece, 2009) could be read as a tear in the fabric of Oedipal–Antigonean genealogy vis-à-vis the epistemological matrix of ownership and (dis)possession. Much too simply, in this film, Strella, a transsexual sex worker, has an affair with Yiorgos, a man struggling to start his life over (and "live his myth" in Athens, according to the 2004 advertising campaign of the Greek National Tourism Organization[2]), who turns out to be her father. Strella comes to make her body "her own" in disowning the gendered and heteronormative certainties of Oedipal kinship and love. Her body performatively incorporates the feminine: her penis is refigured as a site of transfer, specularized and spectralized, providing for an articulation of another bodily materiality and affectivity. The phallus is never merely one's own.

In *Strella*, queer genealogy troubles and redefines dominant histories of kinship, nation, memory, desire, and sexual alliance. The riveting scene of the revelation of the transgender secret – a scene that plays cinematographically with light and shadows, bodies and specters – de-mythifies and re-mythifies a desire for recognition that lays bare the limits of the representable and the effaceable and defies the elementary structures of kinship intelligibility. In the scene of Strella's coming-out as transgendered to her lover/father, the Law of the Father is displaced just as the two lovers (male father and transgender child) are emerging in a post-Oedipal symbolic order, beyond genealogical inheritance and disinheritance, beyond possession and dispossession. In this scene, the multiple figures of Oedipus are re-enacted: the abandoned infant and the triumphant sovereign, autonomous and dispossessed. Both Strella and Yiorgos get co-implicated in a process of re-membering and re-possessing the traumatic historicity of dispossessing desire. They re-embody each other; they are in each other's place and yet dislocated. Strella refigures the infancy she has suffered; Yiorgos is called upon to finally "see," to recognize what has remained misrecognized, dissociations and dispossessions that have lain dormant for a long time.

But let me add here that in the myth, not only Oedipus, but also the Sphinx, the sexually indeterminate subhuman monstrosity, is there to prompt the subjects to the precarious enterprise of recollecting their own selves. In inhabiting both animality and humanity, as well as both masculinity and femininity, the Sphinx's undetermined body-form defies categorical taxonomies and pushes past the intelligible order of bodily subjectivity. Sitting on a high rock and posing a riddle to all who passed, the winged animal and serial killer devours those who do not heed "her" enigmatic discourse, the call of the stranger. The Sphinx's "perverse orality" provides the site where the association of homosexual oral eroticism with primitive (that is, cannibalistic) humanity is enacted (as in Freud's "oral or cannibalistic phase"). As soon as Oedipus responds to her riddle ("What is the creature that walks on four legs in the morning, two legs at noon and three in the evening?") with the answer "Man," she flings herself into the sea and perishes. The volatile figure of the Sphinx must fall before she flies to acts of subversion; she must be overthrown before she overthrows established order. In fact, I would propose that the Sphinx might stand here as an ambiguous, hyperbolic impersonation of Antigone–Oedipus' incest-born, manly daughter who uses proper names improperly and who stands against the intelligibility of *genos*.

JB: A very important point!

AA: So, the universalized foundational structures of kinship are confounded in *Strella*. What is at stake here is not the mere inclusion of those previously rendered alien to or unable of kin ties, but rather a rupturing in the terms of the intelligible. This opening of kinship intelligibility to cultural contestation evades the risk you outline in "Quandaries of the Incest Taboo," of "demeaning the claims made about incestuous practices that clearly are traumatic in nonnecessary and unacceptable ways."[3] Instead, it opens up possibilities for modes of life which have no intelligible place in the heteronormative structures of kinship. Such possibilities, not counting on state-sanctioned legal recognition, involve continuous discursive and affective shifts in the normative terms of gender, sexual alliance, relatedness, parenting, as well as in what constitutes life, the human, and politics itself. This opening performs a constant and insistent politics of troubling: trouble in the political, as it works at the most intricate and profound layers of selves and lives. As such, it is not reducible to a liberal framework of calculable toleration or typical, condescending forms of recognition whose main aim is to extend regulatory control over the intelligibility of subjects.

JB: I think that *Strella* is perhaps the most important cultural contribution in recent years to thinking about oedipalization within queer kinship, as well as about contemporary challenges to understandings of sexuality and kinship, all through a meditation on very contemporary modes of living and loving that nevertheless draw on ancient norms. After Strella confesses to her ailing friend that she has become lovers with her father without his understanding that she is his son, the aging queen warns her that she cannot mess with ancient taboos. This queen paradoxically becomes a kind of Teiresias who sees the past in the present and the future catastrophe that will follow from not heeding the lessons of the past. We are here, of course, prepared for "tragedy": we expect the catastrophic conclusion that follows from a blind passion. But, in fact, the passion is not blind but rather "knowing," since Strella understands that the man who becomes her lover is also her father. Indeed, Strella gives new meaning to Jane Gallop's title *The Daughter's Seduction!*[4] Although manifesting some reluctance at first (offering him chips to eat in the place of her body when they find each other in an erotic scene on her motel bed), she gives way to the desire, breaking the "rule" prohibiting incest and keeping her father blind to the taboo he crosses. On the one hand, we can say that she is contesting the rules of incest that are understood to support the institutions of kinship, seeking to recover and reclaim the father she lost at an early age to prison. Indeed, the violent crime for which he paid was arguably a crime of jealous passion directed against a man he thought was consorting with his son. When Strella reappears in his life as transgendered, he does not recognize her as his son, so his blindness is essential to the crossing of the taboo that he undertakes. And yet, we have to deal with the fact that Strella herself is and is not blind – she sees who Yiorgos is, knows who he is, and in fact arranges for him to stay blind while she pursues her passion, reclaiming him as her lover. What we end up "seeing" is that in a way the father has always been the lover, so something of that prior and constituting passion is literalized in the action of the plot and rendered graphic in the scenes of love-making. The outing of the father–son relationship poses a profound question for them. Though the father reacts with rage after he understands what he has done, he starts to reconsider the rules that are said

to govern human sexuality and kinship, and even returns
to Strella with a sexual proposition, which she refuses.
But when she refuses it, it is not in the name of the Law,
but in an effort to keep him, an effort not to lose this
father again. Indeed, a specter of unmanageable loss
pervades the film, and it proves to be more primary than
any fear or idealization of the Law. And though we
might expect that the fear of loss would follow directly
from breaking the taboo (and later in the film it does),
it seems that from the start the taboo is already broken
and that the recovery of what is lost is most primary.

And so perhaps something more fundamental than
the Law of the Father emerges here, but we are asked
to understand a formulation of the incest taboo between
father and son as a way of designating homosexual
passion within the elementary structures of kinship.
Strella is trying to recover her lost father, and even after
she nearly destroys the relation, she tries to preserve the
bond in whatever way is possible. Her persistence does
not only depend upon the recovery of a primary other
(though the loss of the mother is emphatically unmarked
and unmourned and may also give us a way of understanding how Strella seeks to ascend to the place of
lover: she is his man, his woman, and so every possible
substitute position).

Of course, some viewers of the film want it to end at
the moment of inevitable catastrophe, where Strella is
walking down the street near the Syntagma Metro dissolved in tears, in an open and public lamentation that
seems to know no end, compelled to reconcile with an
unbearable loss. In this view, ending in tragedy in that
sense is better than to reconstitute the family, even in its
queer kinship mode. After an indeterminate temporal

lapse, Strella convenes a queer assemblage for Christmas: a former lover, the father with his former lover, someone's else baby, odd and stray guests who have been in and out of prison. Still, those who want the film to end earlier fear that this last scene, replete with Christmas, gifts, kinship, and reconciliation, is finally normalizing. And yet others who like this last scene understand that queer kinship has always been wrought from ties between ex-lovers, and that though Strella and Yiorgos have lost each other as lovers, they have remained family, not so much as father and son but as ex-lovers. Indeed, psychoanalytically, one might say that the parent is the very first ex-lover, and that we have to include among "ex-lovers" those with whom we never had sex, but with whom we were bound together from the start by inchoate passions. If family members are the first love objects we are compelled to give up, then families of origin are by definition ex-lovers. And if the final scene is decidedly untragic, albeit melancholic, it is because the thesis that kinship requires the incest taboo has been effectively disputed. This disputation is not an argument in favor of incest. But it does call into question the way that the incest taboo has been instrumentalized to produce a heteronormative framework for both sexuality and kinship. The only heterosexuality in this film is queer, and the only kinship in this film is built upon the decimation of the nuclear family and its rules of self-constitution. So according to the second reading, which is closer to my own, the film takes us through the tragic plot in order to question the tragic conclusion, since the tragic conclusion confirms that the only intelligible modes of sexuality and love are those which have confirmed the elementary structures of kinship and passed through their taboos as obligatory rites of initiation. Although it is true that both Strella and Yiorgos come to accept the incest taboo, it is only because they understand that it is the only way to keep each other. And they do not keep each other through a denial of sexuality, that is, by assuming tragic blindness retrospectively, but instead by becoming ex-lovers, a situation in which the two always will have been lovers, indisputably and irreversibly – a distillation of love in the future perfect.

6
The sociality of self-poietics: Talking back to the violence of recognition

AA: In the previous chapter, our discussion of the film *Strella* posed some questions about recognition as a process which is predicated upon (albeit never entirely constrained and totalized by) the operation of particular norms: norms that determine whether and how I can recognize the other or whether and how I can be recognized by the other, but, most significantly, norms that produce an "I" and an "other" in a relation of reflective and projective co-constitution. It would be interesting to think about how the dialectics of recognition, as defined by identity categories, is potentially decentered in moments of self-recognition and self-determination by those who remain abjected by hegemonic racial, gender, and sexual norms, even though they might be occasionally "recognized" or "tolerated" by formal liberal reason. I am wondering whether the apparatus of recognition, especially in its liberal form (is there any other?), can ever be disorganized or whether it endlessly works to encompass, adjudicate, and commodify "difference" and thus depoliticize and legitimize the differential configuration of subjects, lives, and the world.

To concretize this question, let me consider this scene: Mina Orfanou, the amateur actress who played the transgendered protagonist of *Strella*, responded to a journalist's question "What is the most extreme thing you have ever done?": "My self!"[1] In this performative proclamation of a self that has been undone and redone, the self is not created from scratch in the way of an alternative liberalist "anything goes," but rather opens up melancholically to the multiple and non-reducible singularity of the other (self), the one that is left over and, at the same time, exceeds the onto-epistemological typologies of the recognizable, heteronormatively gendered self. As much as it draws on configurations of a self-authoring and self-authorizing "I," Orfanou's answer "My self!" troubles and repoliticizes the liberal typology of the self-owned "I," as it responds to, and is bound by, the injurious, teratological implication ("the most extreme thing you have ever done") of the question-interpellation "who are you?" or, more accurately, "*what* are you?" In redistributing the norms defining the terms of a recognizable self (and a livable life), *this* "self-authoring" self potentially challenges the narcissism of normative selfhood and institutes a different sociality. The normative discourse of abjected and adjudicated exception is performatively recast into exceptional self-poietics.

It seems to me that when the "self" (and we know that the self is always in relational sociality and affectability) who struggles for recognition and self-recognition has been violently misrecognized, constituted as radically or uncannily unfamiliar by a recognizable self-same human, then the economy of recognition gets potentially and provisionally destabilized. This unintelligible and uneconomic self (emerging in conditions of alienation/dispossession, rather than in conditions of plenitude/possession and through matrices of belonging and co-belonging) is not an absolute occasion of miraculous, alter-ontological identity, reducible to the regulatory discourse of tolerable and inclusive recognition, but rather a contingent rupture in proper iterability, a possibility opened by a failure to repeat properly, whereby the sovereign position of the (self-)knowing self is dislocated by a call of responsiveness and response-ability.

The question I seek to address here is whether responsive self-poietics might figure a deconstituting possibility in the apparatus of recognition. This question is a call for a critical reading of the dialectics of recognition, a reading that introduces an element of disquietude and that is in conflict with the governmental logics of tolerance, which seeks to govern and enclose ontologically, possessively, the realm of human subjectivity and relationality. In other words, what is needed is not the creation of tolerant and tolerated identities, susceptible to the market of recognition, but rather the destabilization of the regulatory ideals that constitute the horizon of this susceptibility.[2]

JB: I think we both converge here on the important point articulated by Derrida, via Levinas, that responsibility requires responsiveness. Indeed, I think that many of the affective dispositions that are required for political responsibility, including outrage, indignation, desire, and hope, are all bound up with what one wishes not only for oneself, but for others as well. So I have to ask whether self-poiesis is itself a relational category. Or, perhaps, the more important question is: Under what conditions does self-poiesis become a relational category?

I think that Foucault makes clear that the crafting of the self takes place within a normative horizon, taking issue with precisely those regulatory ideals that determine who can and cannot be an intelligible subject. This is why in "What is Critique?" he mentions "courage" as a virtue that is resonant with the practice of critique itself.[3] None of us know who precisely we will "be" under regimes of ontology that we struggle against or seek to displace. It may be, for instance, that as we struggle against the categories of gender that secure contemporary ideas of personhood, we no longer know exactly how we are to be named. We might be understood to be involved in a mode of self-making or self-poiesis that involves risking intelligibility, posing a problem of cultural translation and living in a critical relation to the norms of the intelligible. I think we can see sociality entering into this equation in two different ways. First, the norms against which we struggle are social norms, and they govern us precisely as social creatures. Second, we make ourselves, if we do, with others, and only on the condition that there are forms of collectivity that are struggling against the norms in similar or convergent ways. In other words, we do not make ourselves as "heroic individuals" but only as social creatures, and though "my" struggle and "your" struggle" are not the same, there is some bond that can and must be established for either of us to take the kinds of risks we do in the face of norms that threaten us either with unintelligibility or an overload of intelligibility. The point is not to institute new forms of intelligibility that become the basis of self-recognition. But neither is the point to celebrate unintelligibility as its own goal. The point, rather, is to move forward, awkwardly, with others, in a movement that demands both courage and critical practices, a form of relating to norms and to others that does not "settle" into a new regime. I take this to be a way of opening to new modes of sociality and freedom. This not to say that we do not require recognition; rather, it is to say that recognition is always partial, and that our capacity to practice freedom critically depends on that very partiality.

AA: Perhaps a cursory reading would posit a facile distinction between a "self-centered" self-poiesis and an "other-centered" ethics of recognition. But self-poietics is no more about "the self" than recognition is about "the other." Self-poietics does not concern just the "self" – in the way of heroic self-sufficient individualism or an alternative liberal "anything goes" – but emerges as a performative occasion in an ongoing process of socially regulatory self-formation, whereby under different circumstances the self struggles within and against the norms through which it is constituted; and such struggles are only waged through and with others, in ways that open up to others (including other selves) the selves that are left over and that exceed the onto-epistemological typologies of the proper and proprietary self. I would think that self-poietics, as much as ethics in a certain way, is a possibility whereby the self is dispossessed of its sovereign position through opening a

68

relation to alterity. If we make, unmake, and remake ourselves, such makings only occur with and through others. Our self-poietics take place within a horizon of regulatory ideals that determine who can and cannot be an intelligible self. So it is with others that we assume and, at the same time, potentially dismantle the norms that threaten to render us either unrecognizable or too recognizable.

JB: I agree with you that self-poietics, like ethics of a certain kind, can imply a dislocation of the sovereign subject. But perhaps we can think about the relation between self-poietics and ethics outside the framework of analogy. My understanding of Foucault, for instance, is that self-care and self-crafting are in some ways modes of poiesis. This opens the question of what the material is on which or with which such poiesis works. On the one hand, it is, as he claims, the body. But on the other hand, it is clearly those regulatory, if not disciplinary, norms that enter into subject-formation prior to any question of reflexivity. In some ways, we are talking about how a self struggles with and against the norms through which it is formed, and so we are perhaps tracing how a certain forming of the formed takes place. If we want to distinguish between the kind of reflexivity that we have been associating with the sovereign subject – admittedly a useful trope for our purposes here – then perhaps we can understand sovereign reflexivity as a movement from and to the self that seeks not only to return to itself, but also to shore up its defensive relation to alterity. If I am right here, then we are both in different ways calling for – struggling for – a conception of reflexivity in which the self acts upon the terms of its formation precisely in order to open in some way to a sociality that exceeds (and possibly precedes) social regulation. In other words, the form of reflexivity that seeks to undo the sovereign and defensive position is one in which a certain crafting of the self, even a labor on the self, seeks to reopen, or to keep open, a relation to alterity. So this form of reflexivity seeks to resist the return to self in favor of a relocation of the self as a relational term. In yet other words, the "I" who works on herself, who crafts herself, is already formed by social relations and norms that are themselves in the making, that is, in process, open to crafting. The sovereign refusal of dependency, for example, is still a relation to the other ("I refuse to avow my dependency, and that disavowal is the condition of my self, and even this explanation that I offer to you is one that I will not, cannot, explicitly avow"). So much depends on how we understand the "I" who crafts herself, since it will not be a fully agentic subject who initiates that crafting. It will be an "I" who is already crafted, but also who is compelled to craft again her crafted condition. In this way, we might think the "I" as an interval or relay in an ongoing process of social crafting – surely dispossessed of the status of an originating power.

Even this description, however, relies too heavily on a temporal model of resignification. You draw my attention to the spatial conditions of dispossession and its implications for politics.

AA: In fact I think this account of performativity relies on and, at the same time, potentially dismantles temporal and spatial models of resignification. The very question of an initiating or originating agency (an agency that purportedly *precedes* social regulation) seems to become suggestively volatile in this protean and disjunctive temporality of re-crafting one's crafted condition – a re-crafting already crafted to some degree. If we figure self-poietics as an "interval," or as a way of "spacing" in an ongoing process of social crafting and being socially crafted, we might be able to see how this interval is not reducible to territorialized formations of identity, and thus our attention is drawn to the intricacies of spatiality and its implications for performativity. In fact, we may track both spatial and temporal implications in the notion of dispossession itself. But I think we deploy such figurations – temporal and spatial, that is – in order to grasp the ways in which "we" are called out of "our own" self-authorizing temporalities and spatialities and toward modes of becoming-with-one-another, supra-individual modes that are out of sync with regimes of social regulation and the identitarian apparatus.

JB: This notion of being solicited out of oneself is important, a point surely articulated by Blanchot and Levinas in different ways.

AA: Indeed. The "self" here does not refer to an autological and self-contained individuality, but rather to responsive dispositions toward becoming-with-one-another, as they are manifested, for example, in the various affects that throw us "out of joint" and "beside ourselves," such as indignation, despair, desire, outrage, and hope. These are all affective dispositions that are "owned" not only by ourselves (if, in fact, it can ever be claimed that they can be assumed as "one's own"), but by others as well. Either in the sense of a non-identical relation to the self, or in the sense of political rage and passion, being "beside oneself" means belonging to others, as it were, who are themselves decentered and "out of joint," tied to norms that exceed them, dispossessed in various ways. I think this perspective leads us to ongoing questions of how to politicize ethics (which, of course, is always already political), how to make ethics congruent with politics, how to make ethics a way of opening to new modes of political sociality. Ethics, as we know, despite its insistent claims of relationality, can be self-absorbed and even self-exalting, as in moralistic and self-exonerating modes of philanthropy or humanitarian reason, or as in moral universalism, which is the legitimizing gloss of the liberal politics of humanitarianism. Perhaps as an antidote to these moralizing modes of ethics, we might need to forge what Ewa Ziarek calls an "ethics of dissensus," which would provide an alternative both to liberal predication on individualized, self-contained, disembodied selves and to normalizing, conservative communitarianism.[4]

JB: I agree that it is not easy to facilitate this passage from ethics to politics. As you know, there are those who believe that any reference to ethics is a displacement and/or neutralization of the political. And there are others who want to secure the autonomy of the ethical domain, keeping it purified of politics. But it seems to me that there are some fundamental questions that characterize ethical relationality, and that we see this articulated in some important ways by Adriana Cavarero in her reading of Levinas.[5] For instance, the question, "who are you?" – this question can be posed in the most personal and the most political of circumstances. Of course, in English, we can say, "who the fuck are you?" when someone is in our face or when we feel impinged upon in ways that are clearly unwanted and unjust. But we can also arrive at the question from a sudden sense of dislocatedness and even astonishment: "I thought I knew who you were, but I do not. Can you tell me who you are?" In the Levinasian sense, the question has to remain open, that is, it has to function as a solicitation rather than as a demand for an immediate answer. In some ways, then, the question has to keep itself open as a question in order to remain in the orbit of the ethical.

I think we can see that this question traverses contemporary debates on multiculturalism, immigration, and racism. It is a question that changes tone and form depending on the political context in which it is mobilized. So, for instance, it can be asked from a position of feigned ignorance ("you are so different from me that I cannot fathom who you are"), or it can be formulated as an invitation to hear something unexpected and to have one's cultural and political presuppositions revised, if not upended. The many references to "the Arab world" or "the Muslim world" not only act as if such a world exists as an integral and knowable entity, but they also assume that everyone agrees on what it is, or that a common set of cultural assumptions are indexed by the phrase. There are certainly reasons that are at once ethical and political to ask the question "who are you?" in order to disrupt that assumption. But there are perhaps even more compelling reasons to postulate the question as directed precisely toward the self-avowed "west" by those who function as its unknowable others. Indeed, we can and must consider the question as emerging from within "the Arab world" toward those who seek to render it into a monolith. "Who are you to construct my world in this way?" meaning not only "who do you think you are?" but "how does your articulation of your own cultural position require this orientalizing of the complex world in which I live?" It seems to me that there are ethical stakes in each of these political encounters, and that it is a question not of a passage from the ethical to the political, but of tracking the political modalities of fundamental ethical questions.

7
Recognition and survival, or surviving recognition

AA: The fundamental question "who are you?" and its multilayered personal, political, ethical, and affective undertones of impingement, dislocatedness, and even astonishment, as you put it, underlies contemporary debates on recognition. I think that we are faced again, in a way, with the impasses and vicissitudes of the liberal ethics and logics of recognition. The liberal discursive incitement to recognition as a regulatory ideal and form of managing alterity manifests itself, in a particularly eloquent fashion, in liberal discourses of cultural recognition. Examining capitalist multiculturalism from the perspective of Australian Indigenous people and their land claims, Elizabeth Povinelli has introduced the notion of "the cunning of recognition" in order to demonstrate how the legal, institutional, discursive, and affective forms of recognition enacted in contexts of contemporary multicultural liberalism work to reproduce unequal liberal regimes of power and imaginaries of national cohesion. In this particular context, where national ideological formation of multiculturalism becomes the grounds for a new national monocultural- ism, Indigenous subjects are called on to perform an authentic self-identity of prenational, "traditional" cul- tural difference ("provided [they] ... are not so repug- nant") as the grounds for a viable or felicitous native title claim and in exchange for the nation's recognition and the state's reparative legislation.[1] So, what is this "difference" that liberalism loves to tolerate and incites to recognition, in not only asking but also answering – on behalf of the Indigenous subjects it is purportedly asking – the question "who are you"? What is the liberal nation-state recognizing and what is it misrecog- nizing when it acknowledges difference? What is it pro- ducing, what is it affirming, and what is it violating? And, finally, how do we survive liberal recognition and its simultaneously life-affirming and life-threatening claims for ensuring and protecting life?

JB: It is a fine question, how to survive liberal recogni- tion. But perhaps it is linked with another question: how do we survive without it? With respect to liberalism, Gayatri Chakravorty Spivak once wrote that it was "that which we cannot not want"[2] and I have found myself returning to that "cannot not want" time and again. The formulation implies that wanting is itself compelled by social and political categories, which means that such categories are not only objects of desire, but also historical conditions of desire. It is one thing to say that I cannot not want liberalism, as much as I wish I could not want it, and so to treat liberalism as an object I cannot do without. It is yet another matter to claim that without the horizon and instruments of liberalism, I cannot want at all, that what I call my desire is so bound up with these categories that without them I may find myself not desiring at all (and so not find myself at all).

For instance, when a woman who is raped goes before the law in order to have the crime against her prosecuted, she has to comply with the very idea of the reliable narrator and legitimate subject inscribed in the law. As a result, if the law finds that she is not a legitimate subject, that what she claims has no value, and that her speech in general is without value, then she is actually deconstituted as a subject by the law in question. It is a moment, like any number of moments within immigration politics, when the demand to comply with the norm that governs the acceptability and intelligibility of the subject can and does lead to the deconstitution of the subject by the law itself. Does this mean that we do not turn to the law to prosecute rape? No, and perhaps here the law is something we cannot not want. And this is particularly true in those instances where there are no such laws, or where laws are being instituted that recognize rape as a crime (including marital rape). And yet, in turning to the law, one runs the risk of becoming broken by the law. And the struggle then to regain "standing" and "voice" becomes one that cannot be done alone, requiring as it does collective support, if not a social movement. And when this happens – and we know that very often it does not – we see the importance of grounding any appeal to the law within a social movement that sustains a critical relation to law (and the risks of becoming deconstituted, abjected, precisely through the liberal instruments one needs).

77

AA: I agree. My question how to survive liberal recognition matters only by virtue of this "cannot not want" formulation which is linked with liberalism! We have already started thinking recognition together with survival. We might now turn to what Hegel calls a "struggle for recognition" (*Kampf um Anerkennung*), and especially to the forms this struggle can take given that non-compliance to established terms of recognizability calls into question the viability of one's life. How does a theory about the struggle for recognition need to be reformulated to encompass the power relations that equate eligibility for recognition with the norms determining viable human subjectivity? A conventional perspective on the politics of recognition tends to conceive of subjects as pre-existent human agents who ask for recognition, effectively obscuring the power relations that condition in advance who will count or matter as a recognizable, viable human subject and who will not. In his psychoanalytic perspective on the colonized sentiment, and influenced by Alexandre Kojève's engagement with Hegelian dialectics of recognition, Frantz Fanon, especially in *Black Skin, White Masks*, considered the impossibility of recognition in the colonial context.[3] The indigenous, colonized subject – as a discursive byproduct of the colonialist historical condition, knowledge, and imagination – is absolutely deprived of any of the kind of mutuality that the very possibility of formulating the political claim of recognition would require. A certain self-alteration would thus be necessary for the emancipation of the colonized from the colonial order.

The relation between recognition and survival (always a question of surviving recognition as "that which we cannot not want") is inherently melancholic in its dependence on social normativity. Survival is configured and differentially allocated by normative and normalizing operations of power, such as racism, poverty, heteronormativity, ethnocentrism, and cultural recognition. It denotes the subject's avowal of the losses and foreclosures that inaugurate her emergence in the social world and, at the same time, her reworking of the injurious interpellations through which she has been constituted and on which she depends for her existence.

The perspective of liberal recognition, which is often too easily celebrated as a secure way to the resistant subject's survival and which sees (the promise of) full and final recognition as the end of politics, fails to ask what the conditions of recognition are. Does recognition, and its prerequisites of assimilation, amount to the subject's self-determined life or to her survival as merely living in matrices of self-definition provided by regulatory power? How can political signifiers that designate subject positions in terms of gender, sexuality, race, ethnicity, and class retain their contingency and openness to future rearticulations? To ask such questions, I think, is to keep open the question of how one survives recognition and the regulatory power upon which recognition is necessarily premised, even if liberal recognition is indeed that which we cannot not want.

JB: Certainly recognition is not exactly the same as self-definition or even self-determination. It designates the situation in which one is fundamentally dependent upon terms that one never chose in order to emerge as an intelligible being. So when Fanon reports on the young boy who points his finger at him and exclaims, "Look, a Negro," he is giving us one way of understanding the social constitution of the subject, a way that has within it the power and risk of de-constitution. So if Fanon is to constitute himself in a world in which the language available for his social recognition makes him into a fascinating and debased object of visual consumption, then he has to develop a critique of the contemporary schemes of intelligibility that govern racial constitution. The point is not to clamor for recognition at all costs, to conform to the schemes of intelligibility that register as assaultive, but to examine the costs of recognition within the struggle for survival. As a result, Fanon takes apart the categories, and ends up longing for a mode of address that does not finally rely on social categorization. Toward the end of *Black Skin, White Masks*, Fanon beseeches his own body through a kind of prayer, to open another way: "O my body, make of me always a man who questions!" Why would he want to become someone who questions after he has been assaulted by racist interpellations? He seems to know that he is at risk of closing down, and the prayer enacts and solicits a kind of openness that is at once bodily and conscious. In the line directly preceding, he posits a new collectivity: "I want the world to recognize, with me, the open door of every consciousness."[4] So though he implores his own body to make him someone who questions, he is also affirming the potential universality of that questioning posture (extending then to the young white boy who has entered into the rituals of racist indexicals).

This final address to himself (which encodes a universalizing hope) remains, perhaps, the most insurrectionary of Fanon's speech acts. Only when a self can recapture and scrutinize itself can the ideal conditions for a human world come to exist. But that mode of self-inquiry, that interrogative openness that emerges from the resources of the body, is itself the ideal, and so not precisely its precondition: "Why not," Fanon writes, "the quite simple attempt to touch the other, to feel the other, to explain the other to myself?"[5] This sentence is cast in question form, and it seems that self-scrutiny implies this relation to the other. In the next line, he writes, "Was my freedom not given to me then in order to build the world of the *You?*" We do not know at this moment whether the "you" is the colonized or the colonizer, whether it is also a reaching for relationality.

Self-questioning is not merely an inward turn, but a mode of address: *o you, o my body.* This is an appeal as much to Fanon's own corporeal life, the restoration of the body as the ground of agency, as it is to the other, an address, indeed, a touch, that is facilitated by the body, a body that, for complex reasons, commits itself to regarding each and every consciousness as an open door. If the body opens him toward a "you," it opens him in such a way that the other, through bodily means, becomes capable of addressing a "you" as well. Implicit in both modes of address is the understanding of the body, through its touch, securing the open address not just of this other whom I touch, but of every other body. In this sense, a re-corporealization of humanism seems to take hold here, positing an alternative to violence or, paradoxically, articulating the normative ideal toward which it strives (and which it must refute in order to realize in the end). It may be that Fanon here exemplifies the belief that *there can be no invention of oneself without the "you" and that the "self" is constituted*

precisely in a mode of address that avows its constitu-
tive sociality.

It is interesting, then, that self-definition, or even self-determination, is understood as a question form, one in which Fanon's own body becomes the "you" at the same time as the world of others becomes the "you." The one addressed through this openness, and as this openness, seems to constitute another form of address than the assaultive racist interpellation.

Of course, this discussion has broader implications for thinking about how schemes of intelligibility and norms of recognition are interlinked in both state-centered and biopolitical forms of power. In either case, recognition is not in itself an unambiguous good, however desperate we are for its rewards.

AA: Fanon's mode of address – *o you, o my body* – bespeaks an intense moment in the restructuring of the terms of exchangeability of bodies, events, spectral figurations, wounding words, and powers that frame our finite human condition. It can be taken, in the ambivalence of its sense, both as self-placedness and as a turn to another. As you put it so well, if the body opens Fanon toward a "you," it does so in such a way that the other body becomes capable of addressing a you as well. This is where linguistic agency, responding, and talking back become possible. In the scene that Fanon recounts, where the young boy points his finger at him and exclaims "Look, a Negro," injurious interpellation is also defused, rescripted, and exploited as a site of address and as the ground of agency. The force of interpellation to produce a subject of fear, shame, and loathing undergoes a radical resignification and re-corporealization. In this context of a necessary implication of the body in language, the crucial point is that Fanon entreats his own body, in its figural persistence, to make him into someone who questions, even in – or *especially* in – a scene that dramatizes the schemes of intelligibility that govern, and leave unaddressed and unquestionable, racial constitution and (mis)recognition.

One of the most crucial challenges that we face today, both theoretically and politically, is to think and put forward a politics of recognition that addresses, questions, and unsettles the common perception of the state or other apparatuses that monopolize power as natural mechanisms of recognition. What needs to be done or undone in order to use the discursive space of the state and other normative apparatuses as spaces for articulating alternative versions of intelligibility? Is there a way that non-normative subjects, lives, and intimate ties could be legally, culturally, and affectively recognized but also lived beyond the normative propriety and exclusionary proprietariness that govern the operations of liberal recognition? To ask these questions is not to demand that liberalism open up its horizon of encompassment and live up to its promises and ideals, but rather to allow for the possibility of exposing the regulatory forces that cohere and sustain these ideals.

JB: This all depends on our ability to function as subjects who can instrumentalize state power without becoming subjugated by it. Can we pick and choose our involvement with the state? And to what extent must there be a mode of political agency that is unhinged from state power in order to make critical interventions into its domain? Some believe that gay marriage is precisely such an instrumental use of state power, but the question remains open for me whether the activist effort to claim gay marriage rights is not a way of submitting to regulatory power and seeking to become more fully ordered by its norm.

AA: The risk involved in the case of the call for gay marriage has to do with the extent to which the state is presumed as a regulatory institution that manipulates the resources of recognition in ways that ratify and normalize the given arrangements of desire, sexuality, and relatedness. If we understand the state as an agent of a public reason that determines who qualifies as a subject of recognition before the law, then the inclusive demand for gay marriage is a policing move rather than a political action (to use Jacques Rancière's terms[6]). Thus, some claim, we are left with a conundrum. Without securing state recognition, modes of non-heteronormative relatedness are derealized; they fail to be perceived and imagined as real, justified, and viable. Recourse to the state, however, enhances the liberal technologies and truth claims of governmentality; it consolidates the law's power to name and to inaugurate subjects, to assign recognition, to demarcate intelligibility, to publicly institute and normalize the relatedness that matters. So instead of a "let us in" plea, which often reiterates the operative conventions of the law, other forms of contesting epistemic violence might be possible that unsettle the normalizing powers of both the law and kinship as always already heteronormative. One might ask here: To what extent are the regulatory discourses of the state and the law appropriable by radical strategies of resignification and subversion? To what extent do certain forms of engagement with the state promote struggles against hegemonic norms of gender, sexuality, nationality, and race? Finally, the question remains open of the extent to which such critical engagements are vulnerable to the co-opting forces of liberal recognition.

I wonder whether and how we could think of these questions through the prism of a right that is exercised even when, or precisely because, this right has not been conferred and recognized, as was the case, in a different context, with the singing of the national anthem of the United States in Spanish by illegal immigrants who took to the streets in Los Angeles in May 2006.[7]

JB: Perhaps we would need to consider how a criminal status converts into a rights claim. This can happen very swiftly, and we see it in the United States when the same immigrants who are threatened with arrest and deportation suddenly become eligible for a "pathway to citizenship." It happens in yet a different way for existing citizens who seek to marry others of the same gender. In some states, parents have been denied custodial rights over their children in divorce cases because they are gay, lesbian, or bisexual; and yet, in some of these same states, existing gay marriage rights would seem to contest the pathologizing and criminalizing views of homosexuality found in these family law cases. In such matters, the "state" is not a single monolith, but a field of conflicting trends. We probably should be glad for that lack of conformity and consistency, since it produces more opportunities to deploy the law against itself. It would doubtless be a mistake to say that all forms of recognition are fugitive modes of regulation and signs of unfreedom. We have to struggle for them at the level of law and politics, though we also have to struggle against being totalized by them.

AA: Yes, I very much agree with you that the point is not to dismiss all claims of recognition as impossible, reactionary, or hopelessly bound up with the regulatory norms of liberal politics. Rather the point is perhaps to shift the terms of questioning toward the matter of why some forms of life and relatedness are more possible, imaginable, eligible for recognition, thinkable, and livable than others. So for me, the quandary that lies before us is how to work on matrices of recognizability in ways that might not reproduce the liberal manipulation, adjudication, tolerance, and governance of difference.

I suppose my skepticism about the politics of recognition (rather than rejection of it) has to do with a skepticism about the reduction of all political claims to claims of recognition. I think I am following here Wendy Brown's challenging argument that movements that demand recognition for the oppressed in already existing terms, notably based on identity claims of woundedness, ultimately shore up and reinforce the very structures of domination that have caused the injury.[8] As modern identity politics relies heavily on a moralizing sense of injury caused by exclusion from the presumably "benign" and "protective" encompassment of the modern liberal state, it can end up re-inscribing the injured identity itself.[9] Again, it seems to me that the point of this line of critique is not to reject identity politics and all forms of recognition *tout court*, but rather to expose and trouble the normative terms that regulate and accommodate identity-based claims, reducing politics to claims of recognition.

JB: It is my understanding that Brown is less worried about the claims of the oppressed for recognition than about the way in which injury itself becomes essential to identity under certain political frameworks. There is a difference between calling for recognition of oppression in order to overcome oppression and calling for a recognition of identity that now becomes defined by its injury. The problem with the latter is that it inscribes injury into identity and makes that into a presupposition of political self-representation. As such, injury cannot be recast as an oppression to be overcome. The transition from an emphasis on injury to an emphasis on oppression is one that lets the category of identity become historical; it focuses politics less on the proclamation and exhibition of identity than on the struggle to overcome broader social and economic conditions of oppression. I suppose you are right, though, that recognition is not sufficient as the aim of politics, if we understand recognition as a static acknowledgement of what is. Recognition itself has to be a transformative category, or it has to work to make the potential for transformation into the aim of politics. Perhaps we can talk about some specific examples of how recognition works?

AA: I think you are putting it very aptly when you say that recognition has to be itself a transformative category. Recognition is not an ontological category; it rather works to produce frames of ontology. In this sense, the question that emerges is: What (trans)formations of the political would be required for non-heteronormative desire to become recognizable without consolidating the state's desire to normalize desire in the name of protecting injured identities? The wish to deploy recognition without allotting institutions of monopolized power the privilege to set the norms of recognizability and to confer recognition accordingly commits us to the constant call for inventing new forms of political subjectivity, in the direction of transforming the conditions through which the political is established. So yes, I agree with you that recognition has to be itself a transformative, even self-deconstructing, force. I also think this matter presents an urgent site of labor for left politics and social movements in our contemporary conditions, which must consider how to summon recognition without perpetuating and intensifying the established terms of recognizability they seek to oppose. This is perhaps an important way in which radical democratic left politics differs crucially from liberalism, even left liberalism. But above all, it is a question which bears very tangible implications of life and death in the ordinary thickness of our everyday lives, as the promise of recognition is typically cast as a safe way of ensuring and expanding livability. So how do certain schemes of recognition regulate the allocation of life and death?

JB: Let us pursue this question of recognition and the possibility of living. I agree that the struggle for recognition is invariably tied up with the life and death struggle. Indeed, in Hegel's *Phenomenology*, it is not only that the life and death struggle gives rise to the struggle for recognition, but that issues of life and death remain paramount (are "preserved," in the Hegelian sense) in the struggle for recognition that follows. Conversely, we can see that even the life and death struggle is structured by reciprocal recognition, which becomes the explicit reason that it fails as an effort to overcome differences. For our purposes, I think it is important to note that established norms of recognition bear material consequences as much for those who are intensely interpellated as for those who are partially interpellated or not interpellated at all. In other words, if prevailing norms decide who will count as a human or as a subject of rights, then we can see that those who remain unrecognized are subject to precarity. Hence, the differential distribution of norms of recognition directly implies the differential allocation of precarity. Of course, sometimes persistence is to be found precisely outside the operation of hegemonic norms. When those norms are criminalizing or pathologizing, then it can be that the very prospect of life emerges precisely "outside" the norm, counter to its violence, and through means that pass under the radar of recognition regimes. If norms of recognition establish a being as one whose life is worthy of protection or shelter, a being who is from the start grievable and whose life is, therefore, valuable, then precarity can be minimized through inclusion within a scheme of recognition. But if such schemes are also based on legal violence, or if they reserve the right to kill or to let die (and so function within overlapping models of sovereignty and governmentality), then sometimes norms of recognition imperil the living, inducing precarity as an effect. So in evaluating schemes of recognition, we have to ask what implicit relations they have to the allocation of life and death. In this way, there is no possibility of separating the life and death struggle from the struggle for recognition. It is one reason that in both cases there is "struggle," which includes antagonism, fear, passion, and uncertainty.

AA: We thus find ourselves in the arduous realm of the relation between recognition and normativity. Recognition is an apparatus that discursively produces subjects as human (or inhuman, subhuman, less than human) by normative and disciplinary terms such as those of gender, sexuality, race, and class. When a life that does not figure as normatively human is violated, this violation remains unrecognized, misrecognized, or recognized in an injurious way, through terms that enable derealizing violence.

JB: Sometimes the violation is recognized, but through terms that introduce new problems. This is one of the debates that is central to the new tribunals, such as the Truth and Reconciliation Commission in South Africa, and to other legal processes that seek to provide an alternative to adversarial lawsuits. On the one hand, recognition is conferred on a violation, but only insofar as the narrative presentation conforms to certain standardized accounts of victimization. Or, as is widely reported, the legal process is experienced as a further violation. And even further, the one who narrates the suffering or violation that has been undergone implicitly agrees to give up the idea of seeking legal redress for the crime. So we might say that recognition sometimes comes at a cost, and sometimes at too high a cost. On the other hand, if there were no venues for recognition at all, that would be unacceptable in a different way.

AA: Yes, you are making a very important point here, one that alerts us to the significance of the distinction between justice and formal regimes of law (that is, bureaucratic, administrative institutions of law-making and legislation).[10] I think it is critical to consider ways in which formal recognition comes with the requirement of the recognized subject's conformity to certain standardized accounts of victimization and depoliticized modalities of injurability. Such a consideration is relevant to various current contexts of humanitarian governmentality, in which discourses of "victimhood" are favored over discourses of political claims and confrontations. But the question persists, in a way, of how to acknowledge and take responsibility for harms done (including the hurt occurred by, and embroiled in, certain forms of recognition). And it is a question that needs to persist, in all its forceful aporias, without either being converted into a claim of formal liberal recognition or being evaded in the name of the perils, tensions, and even violences implicated in the politics of recognition. This is how we turn, again and again, to the question of relationality.

8
Relationality as self-dispossession

AA: Our conversation on the limits and perils of recognition (you mentioned, for example, post-conflict "truth and reconciliation commissions") seems to be leading us closer to the fraught question of relational ethics and its reliance on articulations of acknowledgement, witnessing, responsiveness, and responsibility. It seems we have sought thus far to approach dispossession inasmuch as it encompasses ways we are performatively constituted and de-constituted by and through our relations to the others among whom we live, as well as by and through particular regulatory norms that secure cultural intelligibility. So dispossession implies our relationality and binding to others – in all its subtleties of anguish and excitement – but also our structural dependence on social norms that we neither choose nor control. Dispossession entails the different and differential manner in which the anxieties and the excitements of relationality are socially distributed.

Taking cue from your interest in Levinas's idea that we are impinged upon by otherness, I wonder whether we could think dispossession and self-dispossession through each other. Being dispossessed by the other (in other words, being disposed to be undone in relation to others) is simultaneously a source of anxiety and a chance "to be moved" – to be affected and to be prompted to act – isn't it? The subject's "passionate attachment" to regulatory and productive power is linked to the displacement of the self-sufficient "I" as a form of possession. Significantly, you have traced in the very process of giving an account of one's self, precisely at moments of unknowingness, an affirmative dimension, namely the potentiality of self-poietics – that is, the narration of the self, which assumes the norm and at the same time potentially deconstructs it. In this context, Judith, you have conversed with Levinas and Laplanche especially regarding the way in which they both conceptualize the primacy of the other as a traumatic event that precedes the constitution of the subject. The convergence between the two probably stops there, and I am not sure whether your perspective is closer to Levinas than to Laplanche. You seem to disagree with Levinas's conceptualization of the address to the other as accusative/accusatory, and your own perspective is probably in tension with the Levinasian assertion of universal responsibility. Also, you seem to be radicalizing a Levinasian ethics in insisting that the ethical encounter is organized in and by the normative violence that reduces certain forms of life to the domain of unintelligible, unspeakable, and unlivable. According to your work, human subjects are not only susceptible to and related to other human subjects, as in the Hegelian intersubjective subject, but also susceptible to and related to regimes of power that regulate intersubjectivity, defining what renders a subject legible, recognizable, desirable.

In this context, I am haunted by the question of how we can be moved *to* the other and *by* the other (as well as the other's life-world) beyond the logic of "proprietariness" – with all its undertones of property, priority, and propriety – when the other is constituted as ultimately disposable and transposable by forms and norms of governance. Further, does the ability to recognize or acknowledge self-dispossession necessarily lead to halting the violences of dispossession?

JB: My first response is that one can recognize all kinds of dimensions about one's own self-dispossession even at the moment that one is subjugated by violence, so I am not sure that "knowing" is a sufficient weapon against destruction by violent means. But my wager is that you are thinking about knowing practices, or ways of recognizing self-dispossession, that are materialized in forms of conduct and action.

AA: Yes, I am thinking about knowing practices and practices of acknowledging epistemic limits in their relation to non-knowing. I am also thinking that one should be attentive to the different ways in which unknowingness is deployed, as well as when and by whom.

JB: For me, the insight into interdependency, exposure, precarity, functions as a condition for thinking about ways of countering violent suppression and occupation. It is one condition among many, and in no way a sufficient one. But it has its moment of necessity, and it may be that, as theorists, we contribute to the articulation of such moments.

I am not sure where I stand between Levinas and Laplanche. I brought them together (against their will) only to point out that for Levinas, in a primary way, we are impinged upon by otherness, and that this defines us as receptive and relational from the start. Laplanche talks about impingement as the way of thinking about a general theory of seduction, offering an original contribution to psychoanalytic theory of this kind. For Laplanche, the very activation of the drives depends upon being affected from the start by those whose touch and sounds produce the first and overwhelming instances of an ambient human world. Levinas talks about "persecution" as the primary relation to the other, and this usually alarms relational psychoanalysts, and understandably so. But what he means by this is that we are not given any choice at the beginning about what will impress itself upon us, or about how that impression will be registered and translated. These are domains of radical impressionability and receptivity that are prior to all choice and deliberation. And they are not just characteristic of infancy or other primary philosophical forms of experience. They recur throughout life as part of a not fully articulate sensibility. But perhaps most importantly, this sensibility is neither mine nor yours. It is not a possession, but a way of being comported toward another, already in the hands of the other, and so a mode of dispossession. To refer to "sensibility" in this sense is to refer to a constitutive relation to a sensuous outside, one without which none of us can survive.

Although Levinas would not be interested in contingent social norms, he nevertheless gives us a way of understanding ourselves as "addressed" by such norms at a level that is not fully conscious or volitional. And though Laplanche in his later work does take up the categories of gender and sexuality, he does not think through the implications of gender assignment as a kind of primary interpellation, a kind of cultural "noise" that has to be translated and understood, and rarely is. What interests me most is to think about how various vectors of power, including social norms and modes of discriminating among grievable lives, get registered at the level of primary sensibility, taking hold in spite of us, animating us, and forming a nearly involuntary dimension of our somatic lives. It is awkward to consider ourselves as answerable to interpellations that we barely understand, but I gather that this is the twin genius of Althusser and Kafka. If we are to make "interventions" at this level – what you yourself have identified as a form of regulatory power that operates in the formation of the subject itself – then we will have to ask what form power takes in the nearly involuntary domains of somatic and sexual life and what kinds of interventions are possible from there, in there.

9
Uncounted bodies, incalculable performativity

AA: I am very interested in what you phrased as the "nearly involuntary dimension of our somatic lives." Normative ontologies of the body work to judge, adjudicate, and demarcate which bodies matter. The body-in-history implies a constitutive relation – including the forces of vulnerability, exhaustion, endurance, persistence, and resistance – to the social norms that constitute us as intelligible or unintelligible. You have called us to rethink the materiality of bodies in terms of processes of social mattering that are regulated by normative and idealized fictions of what counts as livable body. In various forms of racism and land dispossession, as well as in neoliberal forms of governance through market assessments, social mattering emerges as an apparatus that regulates contemporary processes of making live and letting die. We might rethink social mattering and the counting of bodies in terms of such exigencies.

JB: Yes, but we have to be careful what we mean by "fiction" (some readers have misunderstood this): this is meant to suggest a certain form of idealization that is historically effective. It is not precisely a "lie" or an "illusion"; it is a materialized form of an ideal that acquires historical efficacy.

AA: Admittedly, it is always important to clarify this. The point is that gender, for example, like sexuality, is not an essential truth derived from the body's materiality but rather a repeated materialization of forms within a regulatory matrix that works to produce the appearance of substance. I think what is also interesting about regulatory fictions, or regulatory ideals, is that no one can really embody them, despite the reigning urge to do so. They wield significant power and efficacy as they congeal over time to produce – or, to materialize – the effect of substance as the "natural" grounds of identity coherence. So they retain a complicated position vis-à-vis corporeal materiality.

It might be interesting for our purposes to take a closer look at the ways in which a theorization of corporeal vulnerability engages with the genealogy of feminist and queer struggles for corporeal self-determination. Second-wave feminism has fought for the right of women to "own" their bodies, and we continue, of course, to claim such rights of autonomy. Queer activists struggle for the right of lesbian, gay, bi, trans, intersex, and queer people to bodily integrity and affective livelihood. How then might ideas of corporeal vulnerability resonate with social-movement strategies and political claims of corporeal autonomy and self-determination? How do we fight for the right to be and to matter corporeally when our bodies are battlefields that are never simply our own – never entirely under our individual control? It is my understanding that to answer these questions requires insistence on the politics of performativity: norms, names, signs, practices, and regulatory fictions can be invoked, cited anew, and challenged at once. Therefore, corporeal vulnerability enables (rather than undermines) claims of self-determination, and we must claim rights of bodily integrity even if our bodies are never simply our own.

So it seems to me that there is a powerful resonance at play in these questions, rather than a mere contradiction. The "I" articulated, claimed, or defended by those dispossessed of self-determination – those constituted as an impropriety – bears the burden and the responsibility of injurious and unjust genealogies alongside its aspirations to freedom. So the question is not how to articulate aspirations to self-determination without seeking recourse to the grand narrative of the self-contained, self-sufficient individual, but rather how to do it within and against this normative grand narrative, how to do it critically, differently. To ask and answer the question of how we might still articulate normative aspirations to political self-determination – taking into account the relational, ec-static, and even propertyless character of human subjectivity but also the foreclosures through which this is distributed and delimited – is to engage with a politics of performativity. I take it that this is the whole point of the performative in the political: the struggle with the norm, a struggle implicated in that which it seeks to contest. Perhaps there can be no political struggle for the possibility of living (and not merely or barely surviving) that does not involve the struggle with and within the normative matrices that determine who deserves a livable life, whose life counts.

JB: Yes, maybe we can say such a political struggle is one "within and against" the normative matrices that condition who can become a "who" in the domain of the livable. At least in English, to "count" is both to matter and to be subject to an arithmetical calculus. This, by the way, can be extended to the category of "civilian casualties" in war, especially in places like Gaza, where the very "countability" of civilian deaths has produced a legal crisis. One might think that counting is among the easiest of ordering procedures, but it turns out that numbers are very controversial. Under conditions in which every member of the population is cast as an "enemy," there are no stray victims of gunfire. The civilian casualty is actually calculated to be within the aim of the instrument of military destruction. In Israel, the human rights group Btselem was charged with treason for publishing the numbers of Palestinians killed in the last war against Gaza (a war that is, in some sense, perpetual). So we have to ask, under what conditions do numbers count, and under what conditions are numbers uncountable? The duality of number and significance does not leave us. My sense is that we cannot calculate the value of life, but that we have to find a way of interpreting numbers that allow us to see who lives and who dies under certain political regimes.

AA: This is a very important point. I suppose this is a matter of asking how the regulatory calculus of countable and memorable casualties might be opposed. We could also rethink "countability" through current regimes of management, whereby bodies are measured and assessed through the governmentality of profitability, accumulation, auditability, and indebtedness. But, to be sure, questioning norms of countability is an unruly occasion – a potentially subversive one when those who do not count demand to be counted, or when those who are measured seek to remain immeasurable. Btselem's "treason" shows that there is a potential for "countering" within "counting." This might be how performativity takes place – within and against – as a means to counter precarity.

JB: Yes, performativity does take place when the uncounted prove to be reflexive and start to count themselves, not only enumerating who they are, but "appearing" in some way, exercising in that way a "right" (extralegal, to be sure) to existence. They start to matter. We can understand this more broadly as a way of producing a political subject, such that the subject is a political effect of this very exercise. The exercise of the right is something that happens within the context of precarity and takes form as a precarious exercise that seeks to overcome its own precarity. And even if it is not supported by existing law (laws that deny citizenship, for instance), it is still supported by extralegal cultural, political, and discursive conditions, translations from other struggles, and modes of organizing that are neither state-supported nor state-centered. In this way performativity works within precarity and against its differential allocation. Or, rather, performativity names that unauthorized exercise of a right to existence that propels the precarious into political life.

AA: It would then be helpful to ask what might be made, politically, of such unauthorized, precarious exercises that seek to combat their own precarity. Coming to terms with this question, one which has become absolutely crucial in our times of neoliberal governmentality through indebtedness, requires the rethinking of performativity and precarity through each other. This conception of performative politics in conjunction with the politics of precarity entails a double movement of performative troubling of the ontological grounding of norms simultaneous with continuous acknowledgement of the unequal and unjust ways in which precarity is differentially distributed as a condition of social ontology.

JB: My sense is that many of the public demonstrations we are seeing now are militating against induced conditions of precarity. And I think they pose the question of how performativity operates as an enacted politics. Sometimes a performative politics seeks to bring a new situation into being, or to mobilize a certain set of effects, and this can happen through language or through other forms of media. But when bodies assemble without a clear set of demands, then we might conclude that the bodies are performing the demand to end conditions of induced precarity that are not livable. Such bodies both perform the conditions of life in public – sleeping and living there, taking care of the environment and each other – and exemplify relations of equality that are precisely those that are lacking in the economic and political domain. In addition, the demands cannot be articulated as a set of negotiable items, since the point of the demonstration is to draw attention to structural inequality and its increasingly dire formations. Lastly, it seems to me that the demand for justice cannot be satisfied by solving particular injustices, even though the accumulation of such solutions can result in structural change. Of course, we see within forms of neoliberalism the idea that individual "responsibility" increases as social services and infrastructures fail, which means that the domain of morality absorbs and deflects the economic and political crisis. And even though that is a pernicious use of morality, I think, as you think, that ethics is a different matter, and that it can provide one point of departure for the critique of neoliberal "responsibilization." It seems to me that morality issues maxims and prescriptions, but the ethical relation is a way of rethinking and remaking sociality itself.

AA: Yes, "responsibilization" is certainly a case in point if we consider that the social therapeutics currently deployed by neoliberal governmentality is very much premised upon a morality of self-government, possessive individualism, and entrepreneurial guilt. It is critical then that we distinguish the calculus of corporate and self-interested "responsibilization," so common to the processes of neoliberal restructuring, from responsibility as responsive disposition that can make possible a politics of social transformation, in ways that cannot be reduced to a mere calculus of interests.

10

Responsiveness as responsibility

AA: In the previous chapter, Judith, you mentioned "responsibilization," and I think that your formulation that performativity works within precarity poses some critical questions regarding the place of responsiveness and responsibility in our ethico-political lives. How is the capacity for response inflected, enabled, and limited by precarity? How is this responsiveness conditioned by the differentially experienced traumas of subjection and dispossession? The politics of performativity entails an avowal of the power relations it contests and depends on; it encompasses "bearing responsibility," as it were, for the power configurations in which and through which we respond to each other. Although we do not own or choose the norms through which we come to exist and connect to others, we bear a responsibility for sustaining them, in a way, even while keeping them open and contestable. The condition of dispossession – as exposure and disposition to others, experience of loss and grief, or susceptibility to norms and violences that remain indifferent to us – is the source of our responsiveness and responsibility to others. Performativity attends to precarity, then. It works to heed the claim of precarious life, through responsiveness, understood as a disposition toward others. In fact, "disposition" – with all its implications of affective engagement, address, risk, excitement, exposure, and unpredictability – is what brings performativity and precarity together.

Responsibility is itself a scene of political contestation, however. Let's consider responsibilization – the appeal to personal responsibility as a flight from social responsibility in the discourses of neoliberal corporate privatization: there are no social forces, no common purposes, struggles, and responsibilities, only individual risks, private concerns, and self-interests – all individually calculable and imperviously self-mastered. As the public becomes an object of disdain, the notion of responsibility is deployed by neoliberal discourses in terms of personal responsibility, self-entitlement, self-interest, and self-preservation, through exemption from vulnerability. Those in need of social services are represented as incompetent, lazy, and, above all, shamefully irresponsible. Eviscerated of social responsibility, dispossession is figured in this context as a failure in the calculus of willful sovereignty and self-mastery.

In spite of, and contrary to, such neoliberal appropriations of responsibility as invulnerable and irresponsive self-mastery, it seems we are agreeing here that responsive disposition, in all its contingency and contestability, can make possible a politics of social transformation. Dispossession-as-disposition thus becomes an occasion for thinking through the issue of responsiveness and responsibility: taking responsibility for one's own position in the world and relationality to others. We might consider what kinds of enabling spaces of politics open up on occasions where we find ourselves affected, undone, and bound by others' calls to respond and assume responsibility. In a world of differentially shared sociality, if we are already "outside ourselves," beyond ourselves, given over, bound to others, and bound by claims that emerge from outside or from deep inside ourselves, our very notion of responsibility requires this sense of dispossession as disposition, exposure, and self-othering.

JB: Yes, and as I mentioned above, this means having to distinguish between responsibility and "responsibilization" – for some, the former is now irrevocably tainted by the latter, but I think that is an error.

AA: Could you explicate the ways in which responsibility does not amount to the liberal and neoliberal apparatuses of moral narcissism and entrepreneurial governmentality?

JB: The neoliberal version prescribes the entrepreneurial attitude and an ethos of self-appreciation.[1] But there is also the Christian version, which underscores the need to care for the poor, a moral maxim that never really questions why there has to be poverty of this kind at all. In other words, in the second instance (and Hegel makes this claim in his "Natural Law" essay[2]), if the maxim to provide for the poor is considered universal and timeless, then it presupposes the eternity of poverty, and even becomes an alibi for its persistence. The solution to this is not to reverse the maxim – "don't care for the poor"! – but to shift the entire problem of poverty to the socio-economic and political level, where we can ask why and how poverty is being augmented at such alarming rates, and how it can be countered.

For me, the question of ethics is always a question of an ethical relation, that is, the question of what binds me to another and in what way this obligation suggests that the "I" is invariably implicated in the "we." So when I am called upon to care for another, or, indeed, to resist a social condition of inequality, or to oppose an illegitimate war or devastating occupation, it is not a matter of finding my bearings in my personal morality or my individual disposition. Rather, it is precisely because I am from the start implicated in the lives of the other that the "I" is already social, and must begin its reflection and action from the presumption of a constitutive sociality. There are antagonisms and incommensurabilities in that field, but negotiating them is the substance of the ethical, if you will let me provisionally wax Hegelian. I think that the idea of the interdependency of lives that are mutually implicated in one another already establishes a principle of equality and connectedness. In a way, I think this interdependency, especially when it manifests in the form of extra-electoral upsurges of the popular will, articulates an alternative to both liberal and neoliberal forms of individualism as well as to unjust and accelerating forms of inequality (Wendy Brown). Thus, in my view, the ethical is neither the moral nor the same as "responsibilization." And if we talk about responsibility in the context of this idea of the ethical, it would be precisely the counter-example to moral narcissism. I do not augment myself with my virtuousness when I act responsibly, but I give myself over to the broader sociality that I am.

AA: This takes us to the sense of dispossession that characterizes the political condition of precarious living: refugees and the stateless, those dispossessed of land, freedom, and livelihood through military coercion and economic deprivation; the *sans papiers*; reserve armies of labor; as well as those rendered precarious and dispossessed by regimes of gender and sexual normativity. Can the ethico-politics of precarious life serve as a gesture of countering and displacing the violence of oppression and domination? Can the affectivity of being "beside ourselves" (an affectivity that, as we have discussed, is both constitutive and differential, or both common and uncommon, in a way) serve as a political resource for effecting new, democratic modes of being-in-common, whereby a certain impossibility of being-in-common is also shared?

It seems to me that, in the domain of dispossession, ethics and politics are not (or should not be) mutually exclusive. Ethical responsibility to others passes through critical engagement with the social norms and resources that render us, or do not render us, joyfully and/or painfully available to each other. We come to respond to one another's requests of one another precisely through our vulnerable strangeness toward ourselves, toward each other, and also toward the matrices that condition relationships between one another. But given the metapolitical appropriations of morality and moralism that abound today, the question of how ethics might act without concealing the workings of power is, I think, a gnawing problem. So, now, through an understanding of responsiveness-as-responsibility and dispossession-as-disposition, we might be better positioned to come to terms with the question of how we offer a self when this self does not fully belong to us.

JB: Maybe that is precisely why we can and do offer it! Of course, we have to pose the question in the ethical way that you suggest: How do we offer ourselves? This is a deliberate and reflexive kind of decision, and it follows upon an analysis of the world in relation to one's own capacities and power. But there is a prior operation of power and language that sets up this ethical question. And we might say that we are opened to a world (or, perhaps, opened onto a world) prior to any question of how we ought best to open ourselves to the world. In other words, it is not just that we find ourselves situated prior to any question of how best to situate oneself. Rather, in order to become an "I" who can question, who can be open to the world (the Fanonian question of *Black Skin, White Masks*), there has to be a set of corporeal and linguistic resources for the posing of the question. In other words, certain conditions for my aliveness and for my capacity to question have already to be opening me onto the world prior to any question of how I ought best to open myself. This becomes most clear when we think about the situation of prisoners who must find ways to affirm life, maintain hope, keep forms of alliance, and maintain the desire to persist. Very often their material conditions work precisely to undermine any such desire, any such opening, any such persisting. So in such a case, the ethical question of how best to open, or even how to remain open, is at once a question of resistance and survival.

It is difficult to stay open when what comes at you is an assault on your being, and this is the risk of remaining an impressionable and receptive being. When Fanon makes that appeal to his own body, he is not just identified with the one who is making the address, but also establishing himself, at a bodily level, as receptive.

AA: To be sure. It is by virtue of its impressionability that a self can be given over. But every time we do or do not offer ourselves, in a social temporality of performative relatedness, we repeat the traumas that haunt our attempt to address and be addressed (while, one hopes, also bearing responsibility for such repetitions). Since we have added performativity to our perspective on responsibility, let us consider the instance of the relation of responsibility to legal culpability. If there is always a long chain of injurious pronouncements and interpellations that precede one's racist or sexist speech act, there is a question, indeed, of where and when a prosecution of the injurious speech act's subject would begin. The juridical discourse of culpability works to recycle the pernicious potential of the injurious speech act while downplaying the matrix of intelligibility that has generated and enabled it. It seems that there is a certain tension between injurious instances and the condition that sets the terms of injurability, as much as they are co-implicated in social temporalities of oppression.

JB: Yes, we are in a quandary, since we cannot say, "Pay no attention to that racist act – focus instead on the structures of racism that make it possible"; we would then end up in a form of dualistic thinking, separating the structure from its instance. The fact is that the structure requires its instance to repeat itself, which is why every racist regime requires its acts of racism, its racist speech, its daily forms of discrimination and exclusion. If we extract the structure from the everyday, then we have produced an "inverted" world in which what happens at the level of structure is more important than what happens at the level of the instance. The same thing happens, as you suggest above, when we only seize upon the instances, raging infinitely and recurrently against the instances without ever seeing the broader institutional and political structures at issue. This is why we have to understand structures as both temporal and spatial, since they have to renew themselves through their instances, where the instance is also always both a temporal and spatial matter. This is why the enraging instances have to be taken seriously, even if they cannot remain the ultimate or exclusive referent for political analysis and opposition.

The moment of injury nevertheless serves as a graphic example of forms of oppression, and the media surely focus on such moments, depending on them to become exemplary. Perhaps the beating of the internet hackers in Cairo was exemplary of the unjust regime and the struggles of those who were calling for its demise. But something else was happening in the graphic instance, which is that the bodies being beaten were also resisting, some successfully, some not. So what we see is not simply injury, but an injurability that is actually linked with a form of physical refusal, and what we call resistance is actually this sustained duality of being exposed to injury and, at the same time, refusing and resisting.

AA: Yes, we are interpellated by and to injurability, but in ways and directions radically ambiguous, which occasionally derail the "graphic instance" of injury and its mechanisms of establishing ultimate exemplarity. The sustained duality you are referring to, the duality between injurability and physical refusal, makes me think of the complex, malleable, and ambivalent ways in which we are interpellated by injurability. We might claim that interpellation is founded on this injurability. That said about the dynamics of contingency and resistance in instances of injurability, we can also address resistance as opposition to the instrumentalization of configurations of injury. I am thus turning to the issue of witnessing and responding to injurability.

The question might be whether there can be a way to answer the call of the dispossessed without further dispossessing them. Perhaps there is no way to answer the call without interpellating the caller and without being interpellated by her/him, without appropriating her/him and without letting ourselves take the risk of being appropriated by her/him. How do we trace the countervailing currents of dispossession in that exchange? Are we supposed to be "at home" in order to receive a call, as it were? Or does the call itself performatively implicate us in unpredictable and unprefigurable modes of relationality and "home-making"? So the question of responsiveness and its implications for today's configurations of the political is also how to think about dispossession not only beyond the log(ist)ics of the self-owning individual but also beyond the humanitarian log(ist)ics of taking possession of the other (whereby "the other" is a misnomer for those with no proper name). I think this critical consideration is relevant to certain current contexts of humanitarian governmentality, where discourses of "victimhood" (including those against "victimhood") work to erase the victims and to conceal injustices. Such a consideration is also relevant to contemporary contexts of intertwined violence, vulnerability, affliction, states of emergency, victimhood, reparation, benevolence, and empathic sublime, which have given rise to new complex and contradictory forms of humanitarian government and non-governmental governmentality, including what Didier Fassin and Richard Rechtman call "the empire of trauma" and Mariella Pandolfi designates "mobile sovereignties."[3] From this perspective, it is critical that we reflect on the ways in which the traumatic event, experience, and narrative might be reclaimed by means of being denaturalized and repoliticized.

In order to concretize the point about the troubling undercurrents of vulnerability, I am thinking of the ways in which vulnerability turns into a norm of regulating immigration and asylum in various contemporary contexts of liberal nationalism. In Greece, for example, women migrants are prompted to perform an "authentic" self-identity of enforced migration and trafficked victimhood in order to become eligible for state or NGO assistance. And in the context of French politics of political asylum, "humanitarian claims" – informed by health-care needs – are being discursively and institutionally privileged over political claims (such as claims of fear of persecution).[4] In both of these empirical examples, discourses of victimization and charity are favored over discourses of political claims and confrontations. In immigration policies, humanitarian reason objectifies and manages immigrants and refugees either as feminized, victimized, and coerced bodies, or as diseased and afflicted bodies. A moral economy of obligatory vulnerability and compassion is deployed as a regulatory norm of paternalistic and sentimental liberal humanism. In some instances of the ethical turn in political thought that has been going on during the last twenty years, configurations of injury seem to enact a melodramatic, paternalistic, and sentimental humanism that typically limits itself to the formulation of moderate liberal claims. At the same time, a conservative biosociality of malaise and compassion (as in the catchphrase "compassionate conservatism" that brands the US Republican Party[5]) becomes central to neoliberal universalism and its moral economies. I am considering, for example, what Lee Edelman has called "compassion's compulsion."[6] Concurrently, in the 1990s a certain rhetorical disdain for "victimization" was elaborated, which has often been deployed as a caustic neoconservative attack against the welfare state: within which particular subjects may be (exceptionally) eligible to get assistance as individual victims and philanthropy recipients. Discourses against "victimization," wherein the "victim" is an icon of pitiful public pathology, cultural defectiveness, or individual failure, are often deployed to degrade and delegitimize individual and collective claims of harm and demands for compensation and accountability. We can recall the feminist protests against "blaming the rape victim" in the 1970s as an example of a counter-discourse to the anti-victim stance. We may also consider various discursive configurations that pathologize and blame the victims, such as accounts that attribute dire economic conditions of poor people to their deficient or inept personalities.

JB: Or, indeed, their failed "family structures" or "lack of strong paternal authority," as is very often the French state response to civil unrest in the poorer suburbs of Paris. That said, I am not sure we can go without the language of victimization altogether, since there are forms of assault and injury that are devastating in their effects. The problem arises only when the discourse of victimization precludes the possibility of effective political organizing and resistance to the cause of injury. It is one thing to unfairly say that someone brought an assault on him- or herself, and so acted to create the condition by which he or she suffers. But it is quite another thing to say that there can be no effective organizing against assault and rape, especially when rape takes on systematic proportions. Sometimes the language of victimization strengthens the rationale of a paternalistic form of power (understood as providing "protection"); at other times, it can lead to practices of organized resistance. So we have to assess in what direction it works, and whose interests it serves.

AA: I totally agree. We have to always make sure that the language of victimization works to address injustice, inequality, and oppression. As you have shown, in the post-9/11 context the role of the "victim" was strategically appropriated on behalf of the United States in order to legitimize its military aggressiveness against Afghanistan and Iraq, but also to suppress possibilities for public critical reflection and discourse inside the US. Your opposition to the instrumentalization of the lexicon of grief within the context of the discursive formation of the nation-state as a victim seems to be premised upon the call for a necessary shift from the first-person, ethnocentric, moralistic, and narcissistically unilateral narrative of trauma to a third-person one – one that acknowledges, and is affected by, the vulnerability of others.

JB: Perhaps, but maybe there is something about shifting between the first, second, and third person that is part of the ethico-political turn you mention. After all, I am not the only one who suffers and resists, and without you, I cannot conceive of my own struggle as a social and political struggle; without him or her, or even "we," I risk becoming restrictively communitarian, including only those to whom I already belong as worthy of consideration. It seems that one has to shift in order to countenance the claims of identity, ethics, community, and global belonging, without letting any of them suppress any of the rest.

AA: One might wonder, then: if the vulnerability of the other calls upon our own susceptibility to previous and current violent modes of *appropriation*, how might we retain a responsive openness to the political futures of alterity, as a prerequisite for the openness of political temporality and spatiality? We have to assess how we can figure the possibility of a non-appropriative relation to those who have suffered dispossession. And further, would not this "figuring" itself be an act of dispossession? One should take the risk, I would argue. What do you think?

JB: Can you explain, perhaps, how you understand this responsiveness? What do we say to those who argue that responsiveness is too "indiscriminate" to furnish us with strong ethical norms about how and when to respond? To what does responsiveness have to be joined in order to become a mode of responsibility that we can call both ethical and political? And how does this possibility link up with a "non-appropriative relation to those who have suffered dispossession?" Are "those who have suffered" at a distance from ourselves? Are we among them, or are they "over there" as the other?

AA: I take your question to pose, in a provocative way, the very important question of community, or, to phrase it differently, the question of precarious relationality. Indeed, who is this "I" who witnesses "your" suffering? Who am I to witness your suffering or who am I to summon your response to my injury? And who are you to witness my own affliction? Are we merely detached bystanders of each other's injuries and injurability? With this line of questioning, I seek to trace ways to go beyond organic figurations of community as a total entity in which people share common things, beings, bodies, or possessions (or common things, beings, and bodies *as* possessions). Can we think of community without eradicating difference, and, with Jean-Luc Nancy,[7] as an occasion in which people share precisely a certain impossibility of being-in-common?

My hesitation here is about a discourse of relationality, injurability, witnessing, and justice that turns "the other" into an essentialist totality, too intelligible and recognizable, precisely since such intelligibility would itself be an occasion of violent appropriation. No doubt, as you say, it is not only that we are hailed or called upon to respond, but also that we ourselves may be among those who summon responsiveness. And "we" are, again and again. But the difficult question here is the one implying a certain being-in-common in the domain of the relation between relationality and dispossession. And there are plenty of different configurations of this relation: dispossessed relationality, relational dispossession, dispossession in relationality, dispossession as relationality, relationality as dispossession, and so forth. I think in this domain, "we" are among "them," with "them," just as "we" are also, irrevocably and irresolvably, without "them." Isn't there always an "over there," as you put it in your question, that is, a process of othering that takes place in the sphere of dispossession?

I suppose my perplexity has to do with the convergences and divergences between different levels, scales, intensities, and modalities of responsiveness to dispossession. For example, when I lose someone, I find myself having lost another person and at the same time having lost something in me. I irreversibly lose a tie that is fundamental to who I am. Who am I, without you? Who am I, after you? I find myself dispossessed from a relation of disposition, dispossessed from a language of address, dispossessed from the capacity (and, perhaps, the desire) to affect you and to be affected by you. This situation reminds me of Hegel's bondsman, in a particular way, and his tenuous and expropriable status: I recognize myself in the state of not being myself, of being dispossessed of myself.

To be sure, our lost relationality does not include only "you" and "me" as distinct and self-contained individuals, and grief implicates us in a sense of community (if not all-inclusive). And it is also absolutely true that a broken interpersonal bond might deprive us of our sense of ontological viability and durability. But can we extrapolate this lost interpersonal relationality onto other modes of lost relationality, when, for example, we lose a place, or a community, or our means of livelihood? I am not quite sure. This is an arduous terrain. Perhaps one way to tackle the question about relationality and dispossession is to try to leave space for the exigencies of ec-static relationality and the eventness of social agonism, while avoiding the introduction of a metaphysical ontology of the vulnerable human body. But I think your work has already alerted us to such concerns. You have shown, for example, that what is at stake in response-ability toward human vulnerability and precarity is not the widening of the established ontological prefiguration of the human (according to the tradition of twentieth-century liberalism and pluralist modes of multiculturalism), but rather, as you have put it, an "insurrection at the level of ontology,"[8] that is, the constant questioning of conditions in which the human is determined by normative and normalizing regimes of intelligibility in terms of gender, sexuality, race, nationality, class. This is indeed a theoretico-political endeavor that exceeds and critically resignifies the scope of liberal humanism and its technologies of determining the distribution of rights, resources, and livelihood. An "insurrection at the level of ontology" seems quite different from an inclusive ontology, especially if we consider the idea that tolerant, inclusive ontology might work as the swiftest way to exclusion. Wendy Brown has developed this brilliantly in her work on tolerating (sexual, cultural, racial) difference as a governmental technique of regulating aversion and managing the limits of the tolerable.[9]

If I understand correctly, your notion of "precarious life," Judith, seeks to suggest a way to politicize social ontology, one that does not configure in advance who counts as human and who does not. This gesture of politicizing ontology, through an "insurrection at the level of ontology," seems crucial to contemporary theoretical and political work. Radical politics does not (or should not) need to be tied to ontological foundations and prefigurations. As much as it inevitably leans and draws upon ontological assumptions, it is also preoccupied with undoing its own ontological frameworks, problematizing the relationship between ontology and politics. We can invoke Foucault here, who showed that the ontological order of things is itself a naturalized effect of political configurations. It seems that radical politics today is faced with the challenge to engage with a certain tension between the "affirmative" and the "deconstructive."

JB: I think Derrida tried in "The Force of Law" precisely to confound this distinction when he turned to a reading of Benjamin's "Critique of Violence."[10] And though I do not fully agree with that reading, I certainly find value in the idea that "the positing of law" can be an affirmative exercise, performative in character. As much as "performativity" exposes the normativity of certain kinds of descriptive claims, it also offers a way to think about how something new can come into being through language. More specifically, it offers a way to think about how new discourse can emerge precisely where it was not already legitimated. I take it that this is the important departure from certain versions of the speech act, and performativity more generally, that assume that it can only "work," that is, be effective, on the condition that established conventions of power remain in place despite being actively contested. And yet when the undocumented claim their rights in public, or when large demonstrations against austerity measures emerge within European capitals, groups of bodies whose speech and actions are not fully separable from each other enter together into established conventions and re-establish them in new forms and for new purposes. I am not saying that such demonstrations are radically new in the sense that they are unprecedented. They can have precedents but still be without legal authorization. Indeed, there are precedents for opposing corrupt or fascist regimes of law that by definition were grounded in no legal right to protest, and there is a long and mobilizing history of such protests. We might say: the performative emerges precisely as the specific power of the precarious – unauthorized by existing legal regimes, abandoned by the law itself – to demand the end to their precarity.

AA: So I think your notion of precarity might imply the constant and irresolvable question of whether dispossession, which deprives certain lives and desires of their sense of ontological viability and durability, renders imperative the theoretical recourse to ontology and ontological conceptions/preconditions of belonging and possession. Given that the point of such a theoretico-political pursuit, which involves and entails an "insurrection at the level of ontology," is not a reassertion of liberal humanism, however, you might want to explicate at this point how you invoke Arendt in your recent work (instead of, say, Adorno and/or Foucault), given that Arendt's work can be taken as typical of liberal humanist thinking in a way.

JB: I hope I continue to invoke Adorno and Foucault as well, and my recent work on Arendt is not meant to announce "I am now an Arendtian!" What I take from Arendt is the notion that there might be forms of political agency, what she would call "action," that require a self conceived as a plurality. This is not a self divided up internally into separate parts, but one who comes into being, and can only come into being, on the occasion of relations with others, and so is "located" precisely in and as the relation itself. At least this seems to be one version of Arendt's view, and it follows from her efforts to criticize political sovereignty and to offer a plural and "federated" version of politics. I want to suggest that there is a "federating" of the self as well, and that this constitutes a specific way of thinking about the relational subject. But more than that, I am interested in how she delineates the domain of what is "unchosen" in life and in sociality, since whatever "agency" is possible and valuable is conditioned by an unchosen realm. She theorizes this issue in fits and starts in her book *Eichmann in Jerusalem*, where she argues that Eichmann and his Nazi cohorts were mistaken in thinking that they could choose with whom to share the earth.[11] Although we can and do choose with whom to share a bed, a house, or sometimes a neighborhood, we cannot choose with whom to share the earth without engaging in genocide. For Arendt, the interdiction against genocide is a consequence of the normative value that comes from the unchosen character of earthly cohabitation. This means that we have obligations to preserve the lives of others whether or not we have contractually agreed to preserve their lives. If a normative demand to refuse genocide follows from the unchosen character of cohabitation, then we must accept and preserve this unchosen dimension of our lives and also realize that whatever actions we do take must be limited by the norms furnished by this unchosen condition. It is of course interesting as well that Arendt, a Jewish thinker and a refugee, refused the Zionist alternative in 1948 that would consecrate the idea of the Jews as a "chosen people." Her argument against genocide was not Zionism, but the embrace of a universal "unchosenness." She joins the "unchosen" against Eichmann, and this relates as well to the important work she did in *On the Origins of Totalitarianism* on the rights of refugees.[12]

Of course, Arendt is not a defender of non-violence, since she herself called for the creation of a Jewish army in the early 1940s and believed that violence in the name of self-defense was necessary and justified. And yet, it seems that we could still ask how to think about the relational self, understood as a plurality, and the self who engages in self-defense. If one defends oneself violently against the prospect of a violent annihilation, is one still in a constitutive relationship with the one against whom one struggles? It is another way of thinking about a vexed and antagonistic relationality that cannot be described or contained by the language of contract.

AA: As you talk about the relationality of the self engaging violently in self-defense and the question of whether s/he is still in a relationship with the one against whom s/he struggles, I am reminded of "suicide bombing," where the fighter (*shahid* or *shahida*) dies with his or her victims, in an absolute thanatopolitical intimacy (intimacy-in-disintegration), which "bears witness" to the relational dimension of self-determination as well as self-annihilation. Perhaps we might understand suicide bombing as the absolute self-excessive exposure to the other, but an exposure that is so self-excessive as to be impervious to the other's responsiveness? Perhaps this is where the "uniqueness" of suicide fighting or martyrdom might reside, rather than in its supposedly pathological motivations – linked stereotypically to the fighters' premodern evilness, which differentiates them from the good and morally developed conscience of just warriors.[13]

JB: Maybe it is important to think about the different ways that life and death are conceptualized within warfare or within contemporary modes of "death dealing," as Asad has called it.[14] It is not unusual to find within any number of religious and cultural traditions a notion that how one dies defines a life, and that singular lives are meaningful only in the context of more general conceptions of life, human and non-human. It seems that even the just-war theorists make distinctions between forms of killing that are justified and those that are not, modes of self-defense that are legally justified and those that are not, and all of these distinctions presuppose that there are legitimate ways that the state may jeopardize the lives of soldiers for the sake of the nation.

Indeed, the US army has always used an idea of "noble sacrifice" to justify sending young men, mainly poor, into combat in which they can and do lose their lives in the course of trying to kill others. We find this entanglement between losing one's life and taking the life of another in all kinds of venues. Perhaps "suicide bombing" becomes a graphic instance of this particular logic under contemporary political and media conditions. But the link between killing and being killed has been a valorized part of warfare for a long time and continues to be so in western and non-western cultural contexts. As much as notions of self-defense tend to presuppose the desire to live, survive, and persist, these same notions, when invoked as military principles, require the repeated sacrifice of life as well as its valorization. So we see something of a life drive and a death drive assembled into a particularly destructive form of militarism in the way that armies work. We find these notions of violent self-sacrifice in US military policy, not just among the Taliban (but there, too). And we surely see this in Israeli recruitment strategies, not just among the Al-Aksa Brigade. They are all willing to be killed in the course of killing others. It makes no sense to cast this as premodern or uncivilized when this combination is found across the militarized field in various cultural forms.

11

Ex-propriating the performative

AA: You mentioned before the various resources with which people and movements struggle and insurrect "within and against" pressing injustices in our times. It seems to me that such moments of collective resistance require taking seriously the relevance of the politics of the performative to precarious politics. In fact, the critical project of thinking about dispossession beyond the logic of possession as a resource for a reorientation of politics takes us back to the question pertaining to the appropriate and expropriative action of the performative. When striving to come to terms with the relation of performativity to precarious politics, one is persistently confronted with the questions: To what extent is the performative determined by the burden of its sedimented histories? Does a performative resignification or reappropriation of a norm, for example, simply take back, take over, or get rid of the norm in its established sense?

A performative is necessarily implicated in the paleonymy of propriation, appropriation, reappropriation, misappropriation, or expropriation that authorizes it and, at the same time, is capable of exposing or even shifting its prescribed limitations. Perhaps a critical labor of negativity becomes the occasion for tracing the possibilities for what you, Judith, have called "performative surprise"[1] – the internal and interminable possibility of misfire of dialectics, whereby dialectics is taken to entail the constant restoration of difference to order. And maybe this way the politics of the performative could be taken to bear the trace of what Jean-Luc Nancy calls the "restlessness of the negative."[2] It seems to me that what is called for here is a conception of dialectics that bears the potential to unsettle its own logic of binary transposability and would thus emerge as a constant and multi-layered battlefield, without a programmatic and definite dissolution of conflict – without a final word, as it were.

Even though norms performatively produce and shape us by default, the possibility of critical invocation and resignification of the normalized order remains open. But so does the gate of the Law, we might add. Consider Kafka's parable "Before the Law,"[3] where the Law's "openness" might imply the perils of renormalization and foreclosure brought into being through new or reinvigorated configurations of governmentality. Of course, this scene of withdrawal of the law, or *from* the law, should not lead us to a reductive notion of law either as a paradigm of a supposedly monolithic and fixed power or as the quintessential means of normalization. As Derrida has suggested, the power of the law lies in its very openness, in its non-materialization. The perpetual deferral of the subject's access to the law is dictated by the law itself: the law draws its force from the constant deferral of its implementation, from its always already wide-open gate. The subject who seeks to access the law is bound to stand, in a position of perpetual presumption and anticipation, always before the law, before the aporia that the law is.[4] But my reference to Kafka's "Before the Law" is guided here by a somewhat different problematic: I want to ask whether we can think performativity with (or through) the messianic. This is an inquiry prompted by your claim in the preface of the second edition of *Gender Trouble* that your formulation of gender performativity was inspired by Derrida's reading of this particular parable. So, I would like to ponder with you the implications of thinking performativity not only through Derrida's reading of Austin's philosophy of language but also through Derrida's reading of Kafka.[5] My sense is that such a perspective implicates performativity in the workings of negative messianism. As we know, in the universe of Kafka, messianism is configured only negatively, through the very absence of messianic redemption: the messianic arrival takes place only on the day after, not on the last day but on the very last; on the one, we might think, that will always be deferred. This configuration of the messianic diverges significantly from monotheistic religious messianism, which perceives the arrival as the total materialization of the Law. Kafka's negative messianism resonates with Walter Benjamin's heretical, non-teleological historical materialism, a historical materialism profoundly inscribed by his Jewish messianism and an unyielding insistence on the unpredictable openness of history. I am wondering, then, what this incomplete, disjunctive, and radically open temporality (predicated as it is on the negative messianic) tells us about performativity.

JB: I have not thought well enough about the messianic within performativity, but you help me here, and I am open to considering how this works. It is true that Derrida's reading of "Before the Law" helped me to understand how the force and promise of law might be an effect of its anticipation. After all, the man who waits before the gate of the law presumes that the man who guards the gate has the power to do so, and he presumes as well that there is some inner truth to the law to which he will, quite physically, gain access. When the gatekeeper claims that the law is only for the man, and that the gatekeeper now, as the man is dying, will close the door, we are left with a double sense of things: the truth of the law will remain forever inaccessible, but also that the truth of the law can only be anticipated within life itself, and that the closure of life is the end of that anticipation. The law is produced and elaborated every time it is invoked in the scene of its anticipation. At the same time, even as the law is produced time and again, it never finally materializes in any full or definitive way. When I first heard Derrida's reading, I understood that one might make this argument about the "internal essence" of gender, something that is everywhere affirmed in popular and medical discourses, but proves to be, within those very same discourses, less stable and sure than it is supposed to be. If there is a sense of the messianic within the performative, it would doubtless be a way of thinking about this anticipatory form of positing that fails to achieve a final realization. If we think about this as part of what I was calling earlier the right to existence, then the performative would be an exercise of articulation that brings an open-ended reality into existence. The "open end" is perhaps a way of describing this indeterminacy that signifies the exercise of freedom outside of teleology (and eschatology). Precarity is crucial here if we are to understand this very exercise as a corporeal struggle for existence, for persistence. Although not all forms of exercising freedom are focused on the freedom to live, none of those exercises can take place without the freedom to live.

12

Dispossessed languages, or singularities named and renamed

AA: We discussed in the previous chapter the promise of performing disruptively – that is, the open-ended possibility of performing within, beyond, and against retroactive recitation, and expropriating limitations and injuries prescribed by it. Thus understood, performative politics, in its conjunction with the politics of precarity and in its engagement with its own precarity, remains open and unprefigurable, persistently and interminably susceptible to the precarious forces of eventness. This unprefigurability, with its promises and its perils, involves us in a possibility of resisting ontological claims and engaging with a labor of the negative. Such theorizing, however, is also concerned to detail the ways in which the labor of the negative must attend to (some would even say, abide by) the necessary possibility of affirmation.

This is how the question of unutterability and inaudibility arises, when the performative exceeds given matrices of utterability and audibility – that is, what can be said and heard. As violences of oppression assume intricate and ferocious forms in the world today, certain dilemmas emerge of naming and being-named, as well as hearing and being-heard. If available language fails to capture atrocity, we are compelled to invent new idioms of "saying," "hearing," theorizing, and acting. But to what extent do technologies of representation produce synoptic totalities of "otherness" and moral consolidations of injury? Gayatri Chakravorty Spivak and other feminist and postcolonial thinkers have alerted us, for instance, to ways in which the wrongs of oppression and dispossession are not audible within hegemonic discourses.[1]

It seems to me that such lexical and representational vicissitudes – including overrepresentation and unnameability – constitute an integral part of the constellation that Adriana Cavarero calls "horrorism" in order to designate current phenomena of political violence, degradation, and suffering.[2] The violences of "horrorism" work by producing domains of both overrepresentation and unnameability. We might consider here the aporetic force of ineffability: on the one side, the ineffable signifies an effect of power in the form of the normative reduction of the erased other to the silenced status of abjection and victimhood; and on the other, it implies the unanticipated event of rupture in the matrix of speakability and imaginability. What happens then to the language of representation when it encounters the challenge of conveying broken human corporeality into the body of the text? What happens to the language of representation when it encounters the marked corporeality – at once all too represented and radically unrepresentable – of contemporary regimes of "horrorism"?

How does ineffability organize the nameable? It seems to me that our critical task might entail tracing the problematic of the articulation between what cannot be said and what should be said, an articulation without guaranteed purity.

A question might also be how to critically address the violence of rendering a person unspeakable without reinstalling a normative regime of speakability in the form of mere naming, bureaucratic taxonomy, or formal recognition. The act of addressing and responding, mediated as it may be by the unfixable and incalculable performative forces of language, exceeds the formal structures of mere naming, capturing, denominating, or even re-membering and bearing witness. This is perhaps about imagining and putting forth the necessary possibility of shifting or disrupting this limitation, even though there can be no question of fully overcoming it and even though (or because?) language always fails us. In the context of proliferating contemporary forms of injurability, we are called, politically and intellectually, to name these occasions and come to grips with them. Most importantly, we are called to capture the singularity (which is always plural, to be sure, as Jean-Luc Nancy has shown us[3]) of those politically reduced to insignificant human matter, or human waste. For instance, in US coverage of the events of Abu-Ghraib, where torture and spectacle converged in an atrocious photographic scene of grotesque degradation, the singularity of the detainees' faces was intentionally erased – reduced to unilaterally exposed and interchangeably anonymous human matter. The erasure of singularity, or de-personalization, is a crucial aspect of biopolitics, much as individuation – in the form of individuated life (*bios*) and the capability to individuate and privatize – is a crucial aspect of biopolitical (self-)management.

JB: To be sure. But perhaps there is a difference between knowing the name and face of every person destroyed and understanding something about the conditions of achieving singularity within a given field of intelligibility. This last is the question of the normative preconditions for achieving grievability. We are perhaps back to the conundrum of structure and instance.

AA: Yes, our attention should then shift to finding ways, again and again, to "name" the normative preconditions for achieving singularity within established regimes of domination. And yet, singularity involves the community, be it a "community of those without community."[4] As Derrida tells us in the *Politics of Friendship*, singularity involves a separateness which might work as an invitation to a (political) community – a "community of social disaggregation [*déliaison*]."[5] But how does one belong when one remains nameless or unnameable?

Let me thus return to the intricacies of naming. I wonder whether, in the face of the proliferation of modes, names, occasions, or social ontologies of dispossession (of refugees, immigrants, exiles, expatriates, LGBTQ persons), we are venturing a return to identity politics, through precisely performative forms of naming. "Identity" has certainly everything to do with injury, in the sense of production of embodied subjects inside the normalizing and traumatizing constraints of discourse and power. The culturally particular forces of identification and subjectivation are inextricably related to the ways in which we come to imagine and recognize a viable life and a mournable death in accordance with given prerequisites of intelligibility. But forging identities around injury is a slippery path, as we discussed earlier; an identity politics that relies on claims of woundedness ends up reaffirming the structures of domination that have caused the injury.

The challenge, then, is how to lay claim to a livable life without taking the embodied subject for granted as a starting point for politics. The very question, "Whose life (and death) matters?" dismantles the ontological presumptions that work to distribute, limit, or eviscerate the possibilities of life in defining the conceptual, epistemological, and political scope of the human. In discussing the relation between vulnerability and politics, you have drawn attention, Judith, to the ways in which social norms determine what kind of humanness can become possible, what forms of life become lovable and grievable. Some critics have expressed the reservation that this gesture, which expels humanism to its limits by casting it as a dehumanizing effect of power, might run the risk of introducing a new ontology of humanism. How could questioning the ontology of human subjectivity – that is, the intelligibility of the norms that constitute us as human – avoid slipping into other forms of normality, other acts of normalization? What sorts of political alertness would this avoidance necessitate?

In your rendition, the global archive of dispossession seems to become an occasion not for a new identity politics but rather for the possibility of forming a basis for relationality or community. Such community would be centered on considering the vulnerability of others and recuperating collective responsibility for the lives of one another. Perhaps what is at stake here is a shift from the (wounded) narcissism of autonomous and sovereign self-identity, which lies at the heart of the individualistic ontology of modernity, to an ethics and politics of post-identity subjectivities, which are consigned and exposed to the exposure, abandonment, precarity, and vulnerability of others.

How can "we" then figure modes of response and solidarity that do not reify "the dispossessed" and thus do not repeat the erasing of their singularity (the destruction of the "uniqueness" of human beings, as Hannah Arendt puts it[6]) but rather allow for a separateness that works as an invitation to a (political) community? Is "ontology" itself undergoing a reconfiguration when we struggle against ontological dispossession? Let me offer this caveat, however: if naming runs the risk of wounding, refraining from naming is not immune to such a danger, either. Would not the avoidance of appropriative naming (the other, the dispossessed, those rendered precarious) produce an appropriative regime of no-naming – with all its implications of idealization, exoticization, romanticization, and discursive piety – and thus reiterate the sovereign logic of silencing? As we know from identity designations, perhaps this is precisely the predicament of names: they are always troubling and yet necessary. We act through them, as well as in spite of them, and occasionally also against them. That said, I wish to contend that if dispossession is to be named and theorized, this should be through a naming and theorizing that takes us beyond both the

abstract generality of alterity and the reification underlying specific incarnations of alterity.

JB: You draw our attention to the problematic character
of naming. To be sure, the act of naming can be a form
of appropriation, and we see this, for instance, in the
Bible, when God extends his dominion precisely through
naming everything in sight (we might say that what he
names comes into sight for the first time). So naming
can operate in the service of a sovereign form of the
performative. For us, the question will be, what form
can and does naming take when it seeks to undo the
sovereign status of the one who names? One way of
starting this inquiry, then, would be to take seriously
the fact that the one who names is always also named.
In other words, whoever uses language to name is
already interpellated into a language, even used by language prior to any deliberative use of language. This
would constitute a general condition of the name that
precedes and exceeds any particular instance of naming,
including self-naming. Of course, self-naming is important, and we surely see this, for instance, when transgendered people struggle with what to name themselves,
how to change the name, how to petition that others
use the name that they wish. In such instances we can
see how the problem of desire suffuses the issue of the
name. Perhaps also with "Strella," no? If I understand
correctly, her name is "star," deriving from the Oneiric
tradition of Greek religions? Calling upon her "stardom"
as well, the name perhaps announces her luminous
status in the world? The "-ella" makes it seem feminine,
to be sure, but it also seems to call upon something
supernatural that diminishes gender in the end.

So perhaps what appears to us, you and me, as a possible tension between particularism and universalism is actually rethinkable in light of a general politics of naming. If we are always named by others, then the name signifies a certain dispossession from the start. If we seek to name ourselves, it is still within a language that we never made. And if we ask to be called by another name, we are in some ways dependent on those we petition to agree to our demand. There seems to be an overdetermination of the social at the site of the name, so however particularistic we want the name to be, it exceeds us and confounds us. At the same time, its generality is the condition of our particularity, the instance of its singular renewal and innovation, some-times a moment of poiesis: "Strella!"

AA: Indeed, "Strella" is a hybrid, invented name that combines stardom – "stella" (Latin) – and madness – "trela" (Greek). Strella makes up a new name to name herself, using a language that she did not make. She reappropriates the violence of social derealization she has suffered as transgendered, through a strategy of self-naming, through invoking other unrealities (perhaps more recognizable in their uncanny unfamiliarity), other ways to be transported beyond oneself. Naming implies a performative which is necessarily interwoven in the fabric of propriation that authorizes it, while at the same time it remains somehow capable of exposing and exceeding its prescribed limits. In fact, the performative gesture of renaming is central to the film as a whole. In the scene in which the aging queen, like a matriarchal figure, warns Strella that she cannot mess with ancient taboos without taking the risk of falling into hubris, she invokes the names of Sophocles and Euripides but transforms them into feminine names. So yes, naming is not only a site of trauma, but also potentially a strategy of subversive mimesis. At the site of the name, tragedy cannot be willed away, but it can certainly be embodied differently.

13
The political promise
of the performative

AA: Our earlier conversation speaks to the subversive potentialities of dispossessed subjectivities, the possibility of becoming embodied differently. As we have already discussed, performativity is about a differential and differentiating process of materializing and mattering, which remains uninsured and unanticipated, persistently and interminably susceptible to the spectral forces of eventness. The political challenge is thus to engage with points of contestation that have the potential to hold intelligibility open to what you have called "the political promise of the performative." To open the political to unprefigurable future significations is to always allow for a performative excess of social temporality that resists being totalized and captured by the authoritative forces of signification. As we address openness to political reinflection (including the reinflection of the political itself), however, I would suggest that we think of eventness not in terms of a single, revelatory moment that comes from without, but rather in terms of performative exercise of social agonism within norms that act upon us in ways that exceed our full awareness and control; a social agonism that produces disruptive and subversive effects in the normalized matrices of intelligibility. Such an inquiry resonates with questions arising in the context of contemporary agonistic performative politics: for example, how to rethink the possibility of an agonistic democracy in our time, beyond a mere extension of the encompassment of liberalism to "more inclusive" or "more tolerant" directions. Or, perhaps more importantly, how to think and enact political praxis beyond and against its normative reduction to a technique of neoliberal governmentality.

Let me try to concretize this line of questioning by referring to certain suggestive political deployments of performativity. You have discussed, Judith, along with Gayatri Chakravorty Spivak, the singing of the national anthem of the United States in Spanish by illegal immigrants who took to the streets in Los Angeles in May 2006 (see above; chapter 7, p. 85 and n. 7). In publicly reappropriating their disavowal in the national public sphere, the protesters exposed and troubled the modes of exclusion through which the nation imagines and enhances its cohesion. Through their catachrestic singing of the national anthem, they performatively exposed and repossessed the norms of visibility and audibility through which the nation constitutes itself.

Allow me to offer yet another example that draws on my own anthropological work on the politics of the feminist and antimilitaristic movement Women in Black in the former Yugoslavia. Undermining the normative associations of mourning with the feminine and the patriotic, these activists' silent street actions bear witness to, and at the same time disrupt, the normative silencing of injurious national histories and disavowed losses. As Women in Black become responsible for the others who no longer speak (the dead of the other side as silenced and thus doubly dead), the languages and the silences of mourning turn from proper "feminine language" into performative catachresis expelled by, and opposed to, the very intelligibility of the discourses of the political. As the idiom of mourning is conventionally imbued with the nationalistic and heteronormative fantasy of the "mother of the nation," these activists undermine the normative role that nationalism assigns to women by mourning for the nation's others, that is, by reenacting the sign of mourning outside the sanctioned boundaries of femininity, domesticity, and national allegiance.

JB: What is very interesting to me in what you remark about Women in Black is the way that their public practices of mourning are not only separated from nationalist projects, but deployed specifically against nationalism. Perhaps also these practices of mourning are separated from their traditional association with the family. So women, presumed to be mothers, who are supposed to produce and mourn the sons who go to die in war, emerge in this situation as antimilitarist public mourners. And they mourn not only for those whom they knew or those to whom they were related, but even for those they did not know, and never could have known. This last seems important to me since it generalizes the grieving at the same time that it makes it more acute. Although the problem of loss is always *this* loss, this person or relative I knew and loved, it is also, especially in the context of war, all those who are injured or destroyed by the peoples and nations who wage war. In this way, the individual loss is not absorbed by the more generalized loss; instead they become inextricable from one another. So, for instance, "Las Madres de la Plaza de Mayo" are mothers, or those who are affiliating with mothers, but they are also militating against the possibility of forgetting the disappeared during the years of dictatorship in Argentina. That amnesia is a historical reality precisely because of the amnesty rules that took hold as "democracy" arrived. In a way, the "madres" – who include many people who walk with them, including men – refuse to allow the "disappeared" to become the disavowed losses of the nation. But they also give bodily presence to the demand, "never again."

It is probably worth mentioning that nationalism can function through graphic and hyperbolic mourning for those who were lost in the midst of conflict as well as through adamant disavowal of loss. It may be that the process of making the lost into heroes is a combination of dramatizing and disavowing loss, since the hero status redeems those losses that are irreversible and so to some extent seeks to reverse a loss that cannot be reversed.

AA: This offers a cue to discuss the ways in which frames of dispossession become a performative occasion for various contingencies of individual or concerted actions of political despair and dissent. It is impossible to address current modes of political dissent without invoking, or "naming" (to echo our previous conversation on the vicissitudes of names), their harbingers. One of the most notable was, of course, the self-immolation of Tunisian fruit vendor Mohamed Bouazizi, on

December 17, 2010, which catalyzed the uprising that ousted Ben Ali after 23 years in power; Bouazizi's desperate individual act of public suicide spawned a movement of collective resistance and disobedience. The unprecedented wave of street demonstrations and protest that led to the Tunisian and Egyptian revolutions was sparked by an act of desperate defiance in response to a violent act of dispossession – the confiscation of the street vendor's wares – as well as the harassment that was inflicted on him by a municipal official. But one should also mention Fadwa Laroui, the Moroccan woman who set herself on fire, on February 21, 2011, to protest being excluded from a social housing plan because she was an unmarried mother – a death silenced by local and international media. In this context of corporeal citizenship, we should also mention Khalid Said, who was beaten to death by Egyptian security forces in Alexandria on June 6, 2010: his mangled corpse became the object of leaked morgue photos that were printed on banners and posters in the mass protests against police brutality and power abuses, and these protests launched the Egyptian uprising. On the other side of the Mediterranean, one cannot but mention Kostadinka Kuneva, a Bulgarian migrant woman and active trade unionist, who was working as a cleaner for the public transportation system of Athens municipality, and was attacked in December 2008 by two unidentified men who ambushed her outside her home and threw sulphuric acid in her face, also forcing it down her throat. That event illustrated the intersecting powers of racialization and feminization that structure the condition of "becoming precarious." More recently, on April 5, 2012, a 77-year-old Greek pensioner committed suicide in Constitution Square, in front of the Greek Parliament, in an act of desperation and protest. In a note he had left, he spoke of his "inability to survive any more," and explained that he chose to end his life with dignity rather than ending up searching for food in the garbage and becoming a burden for his child.

The aim here is certainly not to forge an iconography of "exceptional" or "heroic" martyrdom, but rather to think about how relational and corporeal forms of street politics emerged as a result of people's exposure to, and resistive engagement with, pervasive forms of socially assigned disposability. As street politics today poses questions of dispossession in the form of who *owns* the human and whose humanity is *dispossessed*, my interest is to understand how dispossession maintains an uncanny performative resonance with anti-autocracy fights of our times, fights that seem to occur overwhelmingly through bodily actions.

JB: Perhaps we can also think about hunger strikes in this regard. As we know, those who undertake hunger strikes use their bodies as their resource for political power. The prisoner who continues to eat keeps the machinery of the prison running, so the starving prisoner exposes the inhumanity of that machinery, of those prison conditions, formulating a "no" through bodily actions that may or may not take the form of speech. The hunger strike establishes a prisoner's willingness to die, precisely because the conditions under which that life is reproduced have made that life indissociable from death. Hunger strikes also appeal to humanitarian moral sentiments and arouse public opinion, whereas the usually shrouded forms of prison subjugation go unnoticed. Starving is in this case a form of resistance, and with the help of a media that swarms around humanitarian scandals, it can become a form of public resistance. What is the difference between a public suicide and a publicly conducted forms of death-dealing, either through negligence, incarceration, or enforced isolation? We are asked to consider "death" as what characterizes life under such conditions, but we are also asked, through the hunger strike, to understand the will of resistance. There is no way to be constituted as a subject under one of those regimes (negligence, incarceration, enforced isolation), so the only resistance is through a practice of de-instituting the subject itself. Dispossessing oneself as a life becomes the way to dispossess the coercive and privative force of that form of power.

AA: As we are considering the varied concepts and practices of dispossession, including practices of resistance which involve dispossessing oneself as a way to dispossess coercive powers, I am thinking about the relation of dispossession to disposability, where disposability is understood as a contemporary characteristic of the human condition.[1] I am turning our attention to the theme of disposability especially because pervasive forms of dispossession are posed and countered today through practices that have bodies as their resource for political power. Indeed, the very disposability of bodies operates along racial, gendered, economic, colonial, and postcolonial lines. People *become* expendable and disposable by forces of exploitation, poverty, machismo, homophobia, racism, and militarization. We can understand the politics of disposability as a way of abjecting, a way of killing with impunity, a way of producing the human and its inassimilable surplus. This politics of disposability can be traced in various histories of human liminality, from anti-gay violence and the high rate of suicide among LGBTQ youth[2] to the gendered economies of the border. Regarding the latter, let's consider, for example, the *feminicidios*: recurrent murders of female workers ("las muertas de Juárez"), who have been killed on their way to and from work – electronics assembly plants that supply the US market – in the shantytowns of the northern Mexico border. Over the years, several women's groups have marched across the desert and in the outskirts of Ciudad Juárez where women have been raped, tortured, and murdered.[3] As long as bodies are deemed disposable, found discarded, and remain uncounted, the notion of disposability will be associated with the concepts and practices of dehumanization and necropower. We need to ask, then, with Mbembe again: "What place is given to life, death, and the human body (in particular the wounded or slain body)? How are they inscribed in the order of power?"[4]

JB: Yes, these are crucial questions. And I am mindful as we go through these lists that perhaps there is no one word that describes every instance. Are we talking about disposability? Are we talking about precarity? And how do we describe the particular forms of neoliberalism that we can find in several countries, including the United States and Thailand, in which a body is hyper-instrumentalized for a brief period of employment and then arbitrarily deemed disposable, only then to be again taken up for instrumental purposes for another specific employment task and then once again abandoned? We have to be able to think about the arbitrary and violent rhythms of being instrumentalized as disposable labor: never knowing the future, being subjected to arbitrary hirings and firings, having one's labor intensively utilized and exploited and then enduring stretches of time, sometimes indefinite, in which one has no idea when work might come again. Subjection to such violent rhythms produces that pervasive sense of a "damaged future" to which Lauren Berlant refers,[5] but also a radical helplessness in the face of no health insurance and no clear sense of whether permanent shelter can be maintained. This point cannot be captured by statistics that establish who is employed and who is not, since we are talking about new forms of employment that intensify the conditions of precarity that they exploit.

14
The governmentality of "crisis" and its resistances

AA: Under the truth regime of "crisis," not only do people have to engage in a daily struggle against economic hardship and humiliation, but they are also called upon to bear all this without any sign of outrage or dissent. The current governmentality of "crisis" is enacted by means of the production and management of truth. Through the doctrine of TINA ("There Is No Alternative"), neoliberalism is established as the only rational and viable mode of governance. Predicated upon this doctrine, discourses of crisis become a way to governmentally produce and manage (rather than deter) the crisis. "Crisis" becomes a perennial state of exception that turns into a rule and common sense and thus renders critical thinking and acting redundant, irrational, and ultimately unpatriotic. The boundaries of political space are determined and naturalized accordingly. Thus, neoliberalism is not primarily a particular mode of economic management, but rather a political rationality and mode of governmental reasoning that both constructs and manages the realm to be regulated.

JB: I think you are right to point out how the discourse of "crisis" is already a way to "manage" the crisis. If the media representation of the situation in Greece (and Italy) continues to rely on the idea of "fiscal crisis," then we expect a managerial solution to the crisis, and therefore an augmentation of managerial power. But this is very different from a radical democratic uprising against the massive spread of precarity, on the one hand, and the accumulation of wealth among the increasingly few, on the other.

AA: Undoubtedly so. Despite authoritative efforts to produce a single and monolithic narrative of crisis without alternatives and without heterodoxies, despite state coercion and police brutality, people seek to counteract the sense of helplessness. New political collectivities, such as the Indignados of Spain, the Outraged of Greece, and Occupy Wall Street in the United States, seek to reclaim democracy from capitalism and corporate power. As was the case in different locales and diverse instances of protest, from Tahrir Square and the uprisings in the Middle East and North Africa to Puerta del Sol, Syntagma Square, and Zuccotti Park, the gatherings implicate fundamentally the very condition of corporeal standing in public – in the urban street. It is the ordinary and rather undramatic practice of standing, rather than a miraculously extraordinary disruption, that actualizes here the living register of the event. The very practice of *stasis* creates both a space of reflection and a space for revolt, but also an affective comportment of standing and standpoint. It is such a corporeal and affective disposition of stasis that derails, if only temporarily, normative presuppositions about what may come into being as publicly intelligible and sensible in existing polities.

The calls for "real democracy" (that is, self-constituting as opposed to market democracy), as they are emphatically articulated in the context of the anti-precarity movement, prompt us to try to unravel the foreclosures on which the space of the polis is constituted. When the movement of the Outraged in Athens planned a symbolic encirclement of the Parliament House to stop a five-year austerity plan, the police pre-emptively enclosed the parliament in an ironclad fortification in order to thwart the protesters. The image of the blockaded parliament, defended against the people's demand for accountability, manifested nothing less than the sovereign gesture of closing the space of dissent by delegating the dissenters to a provisional outside.

As this (admittedly very diverse) set of dissenting practices does not emanate from a singular political logic any more than it entails fixed and unified political formations, these movements seem to have a mixed composition, ranging from radical left anti-capitalists and anarchists to eurosceptics and nationalists. Whether such lines within the (mainly horizontally configured) heterogeneity of anti-precarity mobilizations will stabilize or shift, as well as what direction they will shift in if they do, are questions that cannot and should not be answered now. Taking just such a position, for example, the feminist and queer collectivity that took part in people's assemblies at Syntagma Square, in Athens, released statements counseling against idealizing references to ancient Greek democracy and alerting people to the patriarchal and autochthonic nature of the classical Athenian polis, which excluded women, foreigners, and slaves. Significantly, such feminist critique alerts us to the demarcations and pretensions of communitarian belonging through which the space of the social plurality comes into being, especially on the occasion of plural concerted actions and occupations.

Let me add here that this ordinary condition of publicly exposed corporeality in contexts of indebtedness and dispossession is portrayed eloquently not only in the current wave of street protests but also in contemporary art. In her 2010 street performance, "Liquidations," in Rome, Mary Zygouri commented on current debt crises by mimetically borrowing from the corporeal affectivity of political demonstrations. She traversed the streets of the city, roped to a carriage loaded with heavy bags and followed by others, blocking the traffic at times. During that strenuous ritual procession, she made stops in front of suggestive places, such as a pawnshop, where she asked to deposit a pledge. Her enactment manifested the laborious process of engaging with the question of what we can do and undo – intellectually, politically, and artistically – in light of the current governmentality of differentially allocated indebtedness and socially assigned disposability, but also in light of different forms of sovereignty and control, refugee status and statelessness.

JB: Of course, we have to ask what we can do, but we can only know how to answer that question when we understand what is being done and how best to intervene upon those forms of doing, those ongoing processes in which we are, as it were, subjugated and subjectified. Occupying the public space is undoubtedly crucial, but sometimes public space itself has to be created, maintained, and defended against military incursions, or opened up in the midst of securitarian regimes. Sometimes there is no "street" for protesting, since what is needed is precisely streets. So we have to also stay critical about modes of political resistance that do not simply resignify an existing public sphere, but that instead dissolve the lines that demarcate the private, private enterprise, from the public, public security. We have to think anew about threshold zones, including the internet, that sometimes traverse those distinctions and other times retrench both military and securitarian power, corporate control, and censorship.

AA: It is through such enactments of publicly exposed corporeality, in all its passionate and vulnerable intensities, that certain questions are raised: Who is to inhabit public space, to be part of the public, and to lay claim to the public, where "public" refers to a shared affect of comfort and belonging? Does such collective action and affective alliance inadvertently create its own fixed assumptions of placedness and belonging, or does it work to interrogate existing schemes of normativity – be it economic, national, gender, or sexual normativity? To rethink the new contingencies and modalities of agonistic democracy is also to rethink and re-enact the conventional ordinances of participation, divisibility, partiality, belonging, relationality, and cohabitation, beyond linear models of consensual politics and claims of similitude, as well as beyond already constituted categorical schemes of pre-existing subjects ready to undertake action. This seems to be a critical task within the global Occupy movements today: the need to confirm the importance of alliances and cohabitation across established categorizations of identity and difference, beyond the very polarity of identity/difference. The heterogeneity of precarious bodies, actions, frameworks, and affective states invites and requires continuous political work of engagement, translation, and alliance, work that veers away from essentialized understandings of identity and representation, and, of course, that effectively opposes nationalist discourses and practices. I understand that such alliances today are confronted with the challenge to engage in an intersectional political reconceptualization of class, race, gender, sexuality, and ability. But it is critical that we bear in mind that it is not only the Left that is taking to the streets against precarious conditions today in Europe but also, occasionally, segments of the Right and even the extreme Right. So there is obviously a limit to our alliances as we live through historical moments of forced loss. In that respect, the battle against induced precarity ought to be simultaneously a battle against racism, nationalism, anti-immigrant politics, misogyny, homophobia, and all forms of social injustice. I am trying here to gesture toward a sense of proximity and reciprocity that demands a political analysis involved with modes of longing and be-longing in order to reconfigure sociality from a stance of left critical engagement.

So the question of what it means today to take part in street politics as a fractured, dispersed, heterogeneous, and provisional post-identity subject is linked to the question of what or who comes to be capable of being intelligibly, affectively, and sensibly shared in public. What does it mean for one to take part in a plural action of which one is not exactly part, given that multiple collectivities and singularities create a differentiated, ephemeral, incalculable, and transposable social plurality that cannot be reduced to the sum of its parts? What does it mean to take part by not being exactly a part and yet by being tied into the lives and actions of others? In the context of formative and unbearable modes of "being-with" (including modes of unchosen proximity), the acknowledgement that the limits of the sovereign subject constitute the precondition of its agency and the ground of its action can serve a performative enactment of political engagement. Is there anything more politically productive and consequential than the denaturalization of agency as a property of an originating self?

These thoughts sum up a performative account of plural (rather than liberal-pluralist), contingent coalitional politics, whereby performativity is linked with precarity. But I think I would like to insist on the *performativity* of plurality rather than the *ontology* of plurality. What is at stake in this specifically performative account of social plurality is the troubling engagement with the established horizons of ontology within which subjects come to be crafted and re-crafted as intelligible, vulnerable, and relational beings.

At any rate, perhaps this is the spirit, and the lasting value but also the ongoing task, of agonistic democratic performativity: to disseminate its own fixity and certainty, to embrace its situated contingency and provisionality, to suspend definitional closures of political subjectivity and action, and to remain ultimately open to its incalculable potentialities and misfires. Perhaps this vision of agonistic democracy resonates with your commitment, Judith, to a constitutively open-ended and non-teleological conception of democracy – as you once put it: "democracy is secured precisely through its resistance to realization. Whatever goals are achieved ... democracy itself remains unachieved."[1] It might also resonate with a Kafkian poetics of non-arrival. (Let's recall that the "very last day" in Kafka's parable is beyond a chronology or eschatology of realization.) This impossibility of achieving a final realization (in terms of totalization and absorption by an already-established, normative political sphere) is resonant with what we discussed earlier, namely the messianic within the performative, but this time as a specific gesture of radical democracy. What is implied here is not a cynical or defeatist attenuation of struggle, but on the contrary an enactment of democracy as a commitment of incessant contestation: an unceasing engagement with a desire for the political, sustained by its ultimate unattainability. I guess this might sound like a call for utopian realism ... and that would be fine with me.

JB: Athena, I thank you for this incredible description. I think I will simply affirm that I am now thinking about this importantly non-teleological trajectory of new struggles for radical democracy. I am wondering how you see your own philosophical and theoretical commitments coming together during this time in which you are daily living through this extraordinary upheaval. Can you relate what you have described above to your thinking about heteronomy and/or receptivity, for instance? What resources are drawn upon when the "resistance" to realization becomes the "end" that is no end? I take it that this is not a way to describe defeat, but rather a more radical opening of the future.

I am in complete agreement that what we are seeing on the streets are forms of plural performativity. One has one's own story and claim, but it is linked with the stories and claims of others, and the collective demand emerges from those singular histories, becomes something plural, but does not in the course of that transformation efface the personal and the singular. This means shifting from a view of rights that calls upon and re-enforces forms of individualism (and sees social action as nothing more than a collection of individuals), to a social form of agency, or performativity in plurality.

15

Enacting another vulnerability: On owing and owning

AA: As we resolved in an earlier moment of our conversation, vulnerability is about the abiding and vital potentiality of being affected by others and of owing ourselves to others. But it is also always about the potential for injuring, the potential for unevenly distributed and experienced injuries of injustice. However, there must be another way to enact vulnerability, without becoming socially dead from political destitution or subjecting others to a life of social death. This other way to live requires, as you have written, "a world in which collective means are found to protect bodily vulnerability without precisely eradicating it." Envisioning such a world raises, for you, the question of norms. You write, "Surely, some norms will be useful for the building of such a world, but they will be norms that no one will own, norms that will have to work not through normalization or racial and ethnic assimilation, but through becoming collective sites of continuous political labor."[1] I take it that the key point here is the lack of ownership of the norms that are deployed.

This might be a crucial aspect of the critical project to sustain and reinvigorate the politics of social justice in our times: the need to radically repoliticize "belonging," by means of acknowledging and critically engaging its colonial, capitalist, patriarchal, heteronormative, militarist, and ethnonationalist legacies, and by performatively enacting alternative modes and sites of belonging (as "collective sites of continuous political labor"), different from the ones implied by the governmentality of property ownership and self-ownership.

It is through these perspectives that we can see what dispossession might mean with and beyond belonging – the desire to belong or not to belong. I would like to suggest that belonging is not just about being and having but also about longing: perhaps longing for a different way to cohabit the political. Such a cohabitation would involve the performative-affective dimensions that (in)form political desires to belong – beyond accession to (or attempts at) identity categories that regulate the possibility of belonging, despite and owing to categorical imperatives of, and imposed limits to, belonging.[2] I wonder whether we can productively deploy performative (un)belonging as an alternative to the onto-epistemologies of identity in critical discourses of dispossession.

This point might be summed up by the question of whether the ontological violence through which we and others are reduced to improper and propertyless alterity, to fundamental abjectivity, can be countered without seeking recourse to a logic of ontology. I am not quite sure, but I sense there is a reason for trying to avoid doing that. Do you?

JB: I am wondering what is meant by a logic of ontology here. I agree that we have to conceive of a set of alternatives to dispossession that do not reduce a property-owning individual to an ontological valorization. In the same way, there have to be alternatives to precarity that do not reduce to "security." As for property, I am not sure whether I am for or against property as such, but what seems clear in both of our views is that the ontological conflation of the individual with property ownership is part of the very framework that induces precarity. If it is always the individual becoming a property owner who is said to actualize some essence of human individuality at that moment, then the system of property distinguishes between those who own it and those who do not. Indeed, any entitlement to shelter, which is a different matter, would have to be extended on an egalitarian basis. But when property is linked ontologically with individualism, inequality is implied. And when we then think further about the idea of egalitarian entitlement to shelter, it seems that it implies a "dispossession" of the ontology of possessive individualism or other forms of individualism tied to property ownership. In a way, ownership is itself dispossessed from the individual, which does not mean that it becomes collective ownership. It traverses the individual and the collective in a mode that I tend to understand as sociality. It is true that I am willing to call this a social ontology, but that means only that there is no non-social solution to the issue of homelessness and shelter. The need and demand for shelter bridge the specific bodily requirement with a call to organize social and political life on an egalitarian basis to satisfy that need. Once that social framework is established as primary, the rethinking of ownership can follow.

AA: Of course. I am wondering, however, whether we could move the argument forward by asking what it would entail politically in our historical present to insist on avowing the trace of loss that inaugurates one's subjectivity while, at the same time, subverting the dispossessing conditions of territorial displacement and urban homelessness. This simultaneity gestures toward a politics that opposes neoliberal dispossession, which is premised upon owing "ourselves" to others. In light of contemporary brutal contexts of displacement, homelessness, racism, and xenophobia, hospitality is a case in point. The ethics and politics of hospitality involve, or rather require, dispossession: the dispossession of the home (as a provisional sign of affective placeness) and the dispossession of the owner's identity as master of the home. Becoming a host/ess requires giving away one's own identity as master; it requires being dispossessed of everything that defines one as self-owning and self-owned master of the home. This "dispossession" of the identity of master is not disengaged from but rather inextricably linked to demanding the right of housing and other basic conditions of flourishing.

JB: I understand how important this idea of hospitality has become for the thinking of multiculturalism in Europe. But I wonder whether hospitality, understood as an opening toward the "guest," does not presume that the one who is hospitable is an owner, one who possesses the house or home and so has the right to open the door, a right that belongs, in other words, to a proprietor. This would make the guest (like the "guest-worker") someone who is only temporarily dwelling in the same space. And it also seems to suggest that this is a subjective act or gift, one that originates with the individual and even risks swelling the individual's moral narcissism. Of course, it would be another matter altogether "to give one's property away," which is something that I see you as suggesting above. But perhaps even that gesture remains at the "moral" level, that is, does not quite come to grips with the system of property relations, and the differential between owners and non-owners. How would we, for instance, move from the idea of hospitality to the rights of the homeless? Or to the demand that governments supply affordable public housing or livable shelters? It is not so much a gift economy that is needed here, but the development of a set of obligations (to provide housing and shelter to a population) without which "we" as a people would not be thinkable. I am suggesting that it is important to militate for the realization of this ideal, even though that means that I am in favor of "realizability" in this instance. Perhaps the realization of the ideal would imply the de-realization of existing economic and political structures that assume and augment the reality of homelessness. Here again I think we are considering the production of dispensable populations that has become the characteristic mark of neoliberal regimes.

And this brings us back to the problem of precarity. Here I would add the following: the point of struggling against precarity – socially and economically induced and sustained precarity – is not to then value "security," since, as we have seen, it is precisely in the name of securitarian rationality that precarity is augmented. They belong to the same problematic: the augmentation of precarious populations rationalizes the expansion of securitarian regimes. We do not want to accept the conceit that first-world nations promulgate that they are "impermeable" and "invulnerable" while other populations are targeted as precarious. Of course, even that self-conceit inverts, since the same nations that insist upon their impermeability (and here the United States is foremost in my mind) are those that wage war in the name of defending against their own vulnerability. So they "know" that they are constituted by vulnerability, but think that they have the power to instate a radical invulnerability. It is this logic that any struggle against precarity must seek to undo.

16

Trans-border affective foreclosures and state racism

AA: You just mentioned the narcissistic defense against vulnerability that structures the conceits of first-world nations. Indeed, we are in the realm of the narcissistic investments that underwrite racism as a project of producing and disowning the abject. One of the ways in which the logic, or the "psychic life," of precarity works is through regulating and abjecting certain affective comportments and alliances by rendering them either unintelligible or all-too-intelligible, and thus manageable. We can track in the ongoing production of precarious public spheres certain categorical and prescriptive schemes of race, gender, sexuality, and embodiment, which are deployed by normative regimes to organize, induce, adjudicate, and sustain affect differentially. If, in the present conditions of neoliberal restructuring, wider and wider social strata are experiencing material and affective vulnerability and unpredictability, there are also those who have been long forced to accept precarity as the condition of their being and belonging.

We have to ask which affective bonds get recognized and which ones remain foreclosed, unintelligible, mis-recognized, repudiated, or censured, for example by migration policies in the Euro-Atlantic. What does it mean for a nation-state to judge, evaluate, valorize, and sanction the worth of certain gendered and affective enactments over others through its migration policy? The subjection of trans people to the legal and illegal violence of the nation-state is a case in point. Victoria Arellano, a transsexual Mexican immigrant to the United States, died in 2007 from complications of AIDS after being denied medical attention while in the custody of the Department of Immigration and Customs Enforcement. That instance of the state letting a person die posed urgent questions regarding the conditions and norms of intelligibility that render certain affective bonds valuable and others nationally irrelevant or threatening in immigration politics. Victoria Arellano was transformed into a perversely gendered and racial-ized deadly figure, instrumentalized to demarcate a viable, vital, and life-worthy national population. What would it take to make her life, death, and abjection intelligible and response-able? What ideas of the human are implied by prohibitions, protections, and adjudications related to the protocols of Euro-Atlantic immigration?

In other contexts of migration management, the liberal state legislates in the name of republican univer-salism (that is, rule of law, equity, secular citizenship, toleration) in ways that incorporate feminist and queer subjectivities into the mainstream fold of the nation-state. This was the case of the opportunistic and regulatory misuse of sexual rights discourse in the Dutch Civic Integration Examination in 2006 (an examination found unlawful in 2008), in which the immigration service required immigrants and asylum seekers to watch film clips of women swimming topless and gay men kissing, as a way of assessing their capacity to assimilate to "tolerant" liberal citizenship. Through casting women (in fact, *naked* women, as purported icons of western emancipation) and gay people as commodifiable tokens of its paternalistic tolerance, the liberal state power justified both sexism and anti-immigration. At the same time, liberalism instrumentalized women's and queer body politics in order to depoliticize them; in order to dispossess them from histories of struggle and dissent and secure them into the managerial and melodramatic mechanisms of national Realpolitik. Sexual freedom, articulated in the form of moral categories of self-owning, tolerant, and tolerated subjectivity, turned here from a site of ongoing struggle into a normative protocol of security, inspection, public order, and national recognition in liberal democracies. Through this representational misuse, the "Muslim immigrant in Europe" was figured – or, rather, disfigured, caricatured – as regressive, obscurantist, misogynist, and homophobic, while the national citizen was represented as par excellence open-minded, secular, and tolerant. On the level of political performativity, I cannot see any other response to this misrecognition of gay rights against immigrant rights but an allied constellation of anti-racist, immigrant, and queer communities against the violence of precarity and abjection in both national and transnational frames.

———

JB: You have given us a story about a singular person and a social condition at the same time, and your account asks us to rethink the question of precarity as the lived experience of abjection even as we probe the possibilities of performative agency from and against precarity. The anti-immigration laws that would suspend or reject a life in need of medical care are surely ones that seek to regulate who will be able to live as a person within that national frame, and who will not. So rejections, expulsions, and interminable delays are all ways of amassing legal and police power to define and regulate what will be the nation and/or what will count as European (evidenced most clearly in the EU regulations on immigration). These regulations seek to ensure the racial hegemony of whiteness, but also national ideals of purity, evidencing a resistance to the cultural heterogeneity of Europe that is already irreversible, and importantly so. I think perhaps we have to include immigration law as a form of biopolitical control and regulation, one that does not have to sentence a life, or a set of lives, to death in order to let them die. Perhaps this can also be understood in terms of Achille Mbembe's notion of necropolitics.[1] Immigration law in instances such as these is the management of slow death, to use a term from Lauren Berlant.[2]

One also has to track, as you suggest, the way in which the "secular" can sometimes operate as a call for police violence. Any conception of universalism that is understood to emerge from, or be restricted to, the secular is already committing a contradiction and a violence, since the non-secular will not be protected by its terms unless and until they assimilate to the secular norm, leaving all trace behind or, at least, "private."

AA: You mentioned Mbembe, and I recall what he writes about sovereignty as exercising control over mortality. And then you referred to Berlant's work on the management of slow death, making me think of the way she argues that the terms by which sovereignty is thought and discussed often derive from a notion of control based on "theologically based royal or state privilege." Understanding the power of sovereignty in this way obscures the wide variety of processes historically involved in the administration and recalibration of bodies. So too does a notion of sovereign power that valorizes self-controlled individual autonomy encourage heroic, dramatic, or spectacular accounts of agency.[3] This discussion echoes in a way the Foucauldian rendition of the relation of sovereignty to biopower, whereby biopower, in reshaping and resituating (rather than replacing) sovereignty, focuses on making live or letting die. In our present biopolitical moment of crisis-management (whereby economic crises are, not accidentally, cast as contagious epidemics that need to be administered), normative governmentality interweaves with the sovereign decree, and the disciplinary ordinariness of life-affirming welfare protection is coextensive with the selective suspension of the law and the lethal disposability of bodies. This zone of indifference between "banality" and "exception" – as frames of power that shape the conditions of humanness – is the temporality of our ongoing neoliberal crisis *qua* crisis as usual. This discussion poses the unflinching and crucial significance of bodily life – its pains, pleasures, and prospects of change – at this moment of banalized, socially induced suffering. I think that this aspect is rather indispensable to our attempts to invent new ways of conceiving the present.

JB: I presume that in addition to reanimating Foucault for these discussions, we would need also to think more carefully about the relation between biopower and neo-liberalism, and to think about both of these in light of new forms of securitarian power. But maybe this is work for other scholars to do!

Perhaps you know the contemporary Guatemalan performance art of Regina José Galindo, who is arguably most well known for her piece *¿Quién puede borrar las huellas? (Who Can Erase the Traces?)*. In that most impressive piece of 2003, Galindo protested the decision of the Guatemalan Supreme Court to allow the presidential candidacy of Efraín Ríoss Montt, a former member of the military junta known for his participation in political murders. The piece commences with Galindo in a black dress carrying a white basin filled with blood through the streets of Guatemala City. She occasionally sets the basin down, dips her feet in the blood, drawing the attention of pedestrians, and then continues her processional leaving the traces of blood as she goes. The walk ends at the steps of the National Palace, the site where the military dictators ruled, where, confronted by a police line blocking entry into the building, she sets down the basin in front of them, dips her feet for the last time, and leaves them face to face with two bold footprints of blood. The blood-soaked prints are at once the way she "signs" her work, mounts a political protest, and dedicates a fierce memorial to the dead.

The title of the work is a question: "Who can erase the traces?" And the footprints, the basin, and Galindo's own walk enact that question through the movement and fluids of the body itself. The question can take many forms, directed to a range of people and institutions, for instance to the law: "Who do you, the Supreme Court, think you are, such that you can officially erase the brutality of the dictatorship by claiming that this man and his murderous actions can be forgotten or erased, that he can emerge again, *as if there were no crimes?*" The question is also posed to any and everyone who happens to be on the street as she walks: "Will you accept this decision to let this man stand for the highest office of this country and so become complicit with the erasure of every trace of brutal violence for which he is responsible?" The question is also for the police themselves: "Here is the basin of blood that represents all those who were murdered under that regime – will you take this basin away or ignore these very human footprints on the public streets and in front of the government offices where such policies were decided? Are you finally any different from the military of the dictatorships?" Galindo's piece confronts us with the question of whether a regime that effaces the memory of a former regime's brutality is itself complicit with that former regime, conducting a war on memory that functions as an exoneration of brutal crimes.

Many of Galindo's other pieces demand that her audience confront the acute bodily details of suffering, focusing attention precisely on those dimensions of bodily life from which most people instinctively recoil. Such works animate the traces of socially induced scenes of suffering: torture, the slow and repetitive destruction of the body in certain forms of manual labor, sexual violence. More often than not, fluids enter into the scene. In *Confesión* (2007), her body is dragged to an oil drum, where her head is repeatedly submerged in water by a large man. Her body is overcome by that force, and her movements are conducted by his will. In *Limpieza Social* (*Social Cleaning*, 2006), her body is literally hosed down by a blast of water, reenacting the cruel cleansing rituals that happen when prisoners first arrive at prison. By the end of the piece her body, naked, lies doubled over on the pavement, showing what it means to be overwhelmed and rendered helpless by such force. Along with blood-letting and blood-carrying, she lets mucous become a riveting instance of abjection in *Picacebollas* (*Onion Peeler*, 2005).

Zeroing in on those abject or hidden domains of bodily life that most people would prefer not to see, Galindo breaks down the preferences of her audience, shows them what they would not willingly take in, and exercises an artistic force of her own. But the force of her work is to enact and oppose the violent force of the state, the military, racism, exploitation, and violence against women. None of these political concerns can remain abstractions in the course of her performance: her work shows how those forms of oppression are registered on and in the body, what they extract from the body, and how the history of blood-letting washes over those who remain. This is a militant form of body art that seeks time and again, and through different means, to break down the taboos that hold together the amnesiac surface of daily life. An attack on censorship, on the lure of oblivion, the work enacts the traces of memory in and through the body's movement, its falling and faltering. Her body is taken up and thrown down by forces that are too strong to counter. The body is a memory come alive, as it were, one that forces back the hand that might erase those traces. And though in these works the body suffers, falls, and is constrained and overwhelmed by external force, the performing body also persists, survives, showing and enacting a social history, memorializing those forms of suffering and loss against the lure of forgetfulness.

17
Public grievability and the politics of memorialization

AA: Your reference to Regina José Galindo's art follows and appreciates how the ordinariness of living on is often produced and sustained through exceptional, extra-ordinary, and yet unheroizable, modes of endurance. Indeed, such art mimics the intricacies of public grievability and memorialization in ways that show how forms of oppression take up the body, how they are registered on and in the body, and yet how this performing body endures and enacts a different story and a different body politic, a different *mise-en-scène* of the historical record.

Another piece of performance art comes to mind. In a work entitled *Eis to Onoma* (*In the Name of*) (1st Thessaloniki Biennale of Contemporary Art, Thessaloniki Center of Contemporary Art, 2007), performance artist Leda Papaconstantinou engaged with contemporary heterotopias of unclaimed memory in ways that reconfigured the precarious work of re-membering dismembered bodies, events, and biographies – in all their forgettable (extra)ordinariness. Through symbolic acts of laying a wreath or placing votive offerings in the cemeteries of the Jews and Armenians of Thessaloniki, but also in front of a Pakistani grocer's store and a telephone booth in the center of Athens, she acknowledged the forgotten dead of the city but also those experiencing a social death – the migrants, the undocumented workers, the unemployed. Such re-membering engaged with the ways in which memoro-politics is produced through, and predicated upon, a constant contestation regarding what matters as memorable, who owns memory, and who or what is dispossessed of the rights and rites of memorability. The artist performed in places where delimitations of memorability "take place" and are archived in the body of the polis: foreign cemeteries and immigrant neighborhoods, where the ordinariness of the memorialized public order is sustained and yet troubled by silent and silenced memories. The gesture of witnessing *in the name of* others (as in the title of the performance *In the Name of*), especially those constituted as alien to the forms and norms of memorable national belonging, acknowledges and, at the same time, displaces the norms that authorize collective memory through the proper name (of the father and the fatherland).

JB: I think that these questions of memorialization can also be addressed through performance art of various kinds. Regina José Galindo's work is suggestive in that respect as well. Like Women in Black, she also dressed in black when she walked barefoot from the Constitutional Court in Guatemala City to the National Palace a few blocks away, carrying a white basin full of human blood. Her walk, we might say, was precisely an effort to make "memorable" or "memorializable" those who were killed under the dictatorships of the 1980s. Her action, shocking as it is (drawing from tragic traditions in which there is a sudden and disconcerting revelation of blood and death), mourned, memorialized, and resisted all at the same time.

Of course, her performance is a single action, but she acts in the name of the people, both lost and present. Can we return, then, to the idea of plural performativity? It seems to have at least two important effects: one is articulating a voice of the people from the singularity of the story and the obduracy of the body, a voice at once individual and social; another is the reproduction of community or sociality itself as bodies congregate and "live together" on the street. They come to enact forms of interdependency, persistence, resistance, and equality that allow them to create a counter-socius in the midst of hierarchical and regulatory power regimes.

18

The political affects of plural performativity

AA: Returning, then, to the idea of plural performativity (as performativity *of* plurality and performativity *in* plurality), let us try to unravel its political eventness, in the context of recent movements and aggregations in public spaces. What might the agonistic intercorporeality and conviviality of the crowds assembling in the cities, day and night, and protesting against their governments' abuses of power mean for the enactment and the eventuality of the political? How does this alternative economy of bodies offer space for effectual critique of the disembodied and affectively purified subject of conventional liberal democracy? How does this alternative economy of bodies offer space for objecting to neoliberal regimes of economization of life?

As crisis becomes ordinary, one of the questions that we might need to puzzle over here is this: How do we become "moved" by, through, toward, as well as away from, dispossession in our modes of surviving global capitalism and its debt cycles? What does this social passion *qua* collective movement (*e-motion*) owe to the ec-static character of subjectivity – to our being beside ourselves and moving beyond the powers by which we are enabled? In the current instances of assembling intensity, revolt emerges as a reconfiguration of the normative operations of power that regulate the limits of the desirable, the sensible, and the intelligible. Affect, in this context, signifies affecting and being affected by the corporeal dynamic of relatedness, mutual vulnerability, and endurance. It involves being beside oneself: taken out, given over, moved, and moving. Consider, for example, the "Friday of anger" protests in Cairo and the "movement of the Outraged" in the European South. In holding up the square as a node of agonistic sociability, those bodies in stasis and in motion created space not as a static physical location but rather as a contingent field of flows and forces, extension and intension. The public expression of outrage in European cities has been vehemently attacked by various elite commentators as being "immature," non-political, and too emotional, while what is supposedly needed is a rational, technocratic management of economic rates. The political devaluing of passion – in all its assigned connotations of irrational sentimental femininity, uncivilized primitiveness, and an inarticulate working class – is premised upon the normative and normalizing reduction of the political to juridical reason. What the gatherings bring forth, however, from Tahrir to Puerta del Sol and from Syntagma Square to Zucchotti Park, is a politics that involves and mobilizes affective dispositions, such as apprehension, outrage, despair, and occasionally hope, but is not thereby sentimental.

Although the current street-politics configurations involve the body in its injuries and innovations, they do not take it for granted. Instead, they take into account – as well as account for – the multiple ways in which bodies are "beside themselves," dispossessed, comported beyond themselves. The public gatherings enable and enact a performativity of embodied agency, in which we own our bodies and struggle for the right to claim our bodies as "ours" (as we ask, for example, that the state keep off our bodies). However, our claim does not refer merely to individual, individually owned, self-sufficient bodies, but rather to the relationality of these bodies. Taking part in the multi-layered and multi-sited gatherings involves the corporeal vulnerability of fatigue, weariness, exhaustive obligation to pay the debt to capital, the life-threatening violence of profit extraction, exposure to police repression and brutality (including massive tear-gas and chemical exposure), but also a shared affective economy of motivation, endurance, changeability, and vitalization. If the square gatherings of protest seek to open "space to breathe," unprovoked assaults by riot police on unarmed citizens with suffocating tear-gas pose, again and again, the question of bearability and livability. In the affective economy of such aggregations, corporeal vulnerability and revolt become each other's indeterminate condition of possibility. The body becomes a turbulent performative occasion, one that both constrains and enables action *qua* embodied situatedness and extension. Perhaps this multivalent interaction of bodies, in all its affective and political intensities of empathy, kindness, and alliance – but also of tension, distress, or conflict – opens ways for thinking the materiality and affectivity of embodied agency without restoring the body as a hypostatized foundation of identitarian action and agency.

Such a conceptualization of street politics, through the perspective of our disposition to affect the world around us and our disposition to be affected by it, could work as an occasion for thinking about freedom beyond the bounds of liberal individualism. Such figuration of agency requires us to question liberal ideas about freedom, and, more specifically, the idea of the disembodied, affectively purged, self-owning individual as integral to the liberal conception of the free human subject. This also entails asking: What do modern histories of dispossession and related neoliberal forms of governmentality tell us about the liberal figuration of the human subject as paradigmatically and disembodiedly human? What do they tell us about the figuration of freedom as an inalienable form of property? In short, I am left wondering whether these new configurations of political mobilization and insurrection, in their different (but also often similar) ways of being enacted in various regions of the contemporary world, instigate a shift in our habitual ways of thinking politically about freedom through the perspective of bodily materialities and temporalities.

JB: I very much like the idea of the body as "a turbulent performative occasion." And yes, we are left with having to rethink freedom, as many other people have done. I think you and I are considering bodily freedom in its plural form, which involves an Arendtian understanding of "concerted action," but one that must refuse the particular way she distinguished the public from the private sphere. In fact, in many of the street assemblies and square encampments, bodily needs are being organized in a common space, which is not to say that everything about private life is exposed. The tent does provide some provisional shade and retreat, to be sure. But if we ask where and how we find freedom in such instances of "square living," then it seems at once to be a dimension of conviviality or cohabitation, resistance, and action. This does not mean that everyone acts together or in unison, but that enough actions are interweaving that a collective effect is registered. The "I" is not dissolved in such a collectivity, but its own situation is presented or "demonstrated" as linked to a patterned social condition.

AA: I think we can track this corporeal politics of "making space" and "taking place" in various forms of civil disobedience and struggles against contemporary antidemocratic configurations of power. In fact, in mobilizing "dispossession" as an enabling arena for a politics of the performative, even in uttering the term "dispossession" and thus unavoidably reciting its injurious historicity, we must turn to resistances against the ongoing conditions of occupation in Palestine, although we can hardly do them justice. We need, in such a turn, to attend to the intensities that arise every day in the villages along the path of the barrier – the barrier that works to consolidate the annexation of Palestinian land by Israeli settlements and that routinely destroys lives, homes, communities, lands, and infrastructural conditions of livelihood and sociability. In ordinary forms of resistance, or in the weekly rallies against the wall that take place at Bil'in, people insistently put their bodies on the line against settler colonialism, land confiscation, militarism, and enduring conditions of economic and political destitution. Rather than implying a transcendent euphoria of effective will or redemption, "resistance" pertains to the ordinary and extraordinary forces of endurance and survival, emerging from, and potentially dissolving, the political condition of enforced precarious living. And yet, in their ordinary and extraordinary forms of surviving, Palestinians do not merely survive occupation and apartheid (although there is nothing *mere* about surviving), but they also defy and trouble the colonial foreclosure of the possibility to live. "Survival," therefore, refers not to an existential drive of mere self-preservation but rather to the collective contingencies of exercising freedom, even in structurally unfree conditions, that produce contexts of survival as merely, or barely, living.

JB: Under the conditions of occupation in Palestine, we might say that the entire population is unfree, both in the West Bank and in Gaza, as well as in the refugee camps. And we have to say it, to be sure, since the Palestinian population remain under an enduring colonial rule and subjugation. And yet the acts of freedom that emerge from within the occupation include ways of resisting Israeli army guards at the checkpoint, forms of non-compliance with regulations imposed by the Israeli state, forms of border-crossing under the radar, and education and publications, especially on the internet. So there are all sorts of moments and practices of freedom under subjugation, but this does not ameliorate the normative objection to the occupation or the confiscation of property, the expulsions that still continue, and the compromised and limited citizenship of so-called Palestinian Israelis. It is perhaps at this moment that we have to consider whether resistance is a better name for this freedom, since freedom does not emanate from a part of the soul or a dimension of one's nature, but is articulated in its exercise. And in the case of resisting occupation, the specific form that freedom takes is resistance – or, at least, that is one dominant form. "Freedom" itself is a political term, to be sure, and when one reads the sign "Free Palestine," one understands that it is a call to bring the colonial regime to an end and to liberate the Palestinian people from those shackles. But it matters how one sees the transition – is it an entry into liberal political economy, a nation-state status, or is it more simply a "liberation" into self-determination as a political category? Self-determination designates a process whose end is not known (and whose "unrealizability" is perhaps a way of characterizing that ongoing and open process). Surely no one from the outside can prescribe the political form that self-determining Palestinians may craft for themselves, but whatever form does take place, it will have to be legitimated by a process of self-determination. And it will only remain legitimate to the extent that that process remains ongoing. So we can call this freedom, and we can locate the absolute demand to be "emancipated" from colonial rule, but once we begin to think about the next step, that is where we are under some obligation not to conceptualize or prescribe in the name of those who will be making and living that new form together.

AA: This is a really complex matter. You force me to think the importance of promoting critical thinking about the question of the desire for freedom, especially regarding collective acts of political freedom, despite the problems inherent in processes of formulating discourses of freedom. Here lies the importance of Foucault's notion of resistance as well as his creative understanding of the relation between freedom and power. "Rather than speaking an essential freedom," writes Foucault, "it would be better to speak of an 'agonism' – of a relationship which is at the same time reciprocal incitation and struggle."[1]

It seems to me that our whole conversation has had as an underlying leitmotif the question of freedom with others as freedom from the violence inherent in the freedom of individual will. We have been concerned with the political responsibility emerging when an individualistic sovereign subject is effectively challenged and when its constituting difference challenges the prerequisites of proper subjectivity. It seems to me also that it is crucial to work toward formulating projects of concerted action and collective freedom, to enact freedom along with others, while retaining and engaging with the critical force of difference. Aren't we still attached to the urgency and the difficulty of this political project?

19
Conundrums of solidarity

AA: So the question is, how are we to struggle for a desire to exist and to be free, when this desire is not exactly "ours," in fact can never be exclusively "ours"? This question implies the aporia of solidarity as an injurious yet enabling mode of "concerted action" in conditions of dispossession (of property, land, rights, livelihood, or relationality). An example here is the multiple forms of alliance and solidarity – among Palestinian locals, Palestinian Israelis, Israeli dissenters, and international activists – that have emerged in relation to the occupation of Palestine; what is revealed is their possibilities and their limits, their enabling perplexities and daunting shortcomings. Through the solidarity rallies against the apartheid wall, or through the Boycott, Divestment, and Sanctions campaign (BDS), a growing international movement for a free Palestine seeks to affirm its association with the Palestinian struggle.

Perhaps there is something to be learned from such collectivities of political action as Palestinian Queers for BDS (PQBDS), which is attentive to the organic linkage of anti-colonial resistance with struggles within and against gender and sexual normativity. Again, the point of solidarity is not to produce injury-formed identities and determine which mode of injustice – sexual injustice, economic precarity, or occupation – is the most injurious, but rather to make space for dismantling the social conventions and foreclosures that render some lives and desires impossible. Solidarity is unavoidably interwoven in the normative violence inherent in the ways we come to imagine and recognize a viable life in accordance with given prerequisites of intelligibility. At the same time, though, it somehow offers a space for exposing and perhaps exceeding such prescribed limits.

Today's social movements of solidarity are faced with the challenge to build political and affective alliances in ways that allow "ontology" itself, as a biopolitical demarcation of the scope of the human, to undergo a radical transfiguration. If available language of solidarity fails to resist the violations inherent in processes of formulating discourses of alterity, we are compelled to invent new idioms of theorizing, acting, and making coalitions.

JB: I am sure that we are! It seems to me that Palestinian Queers for BDS are mapping the complexity of a contemporary political alliance. It is clear that they oppose homophobia, but they also refuse to accept the idea that homophobia is restricted to Arab or, more specifically, Palestinian domains. So in this way, they have to refuse the uncritical gay and lesbian human rights framework that imagines that it is carrying emancipatory rights from the west to the east and from the north to the south. At the same time, PQBDS would find it impossible to make alliances with Israelis who are not seriously challenging the basis of the Israeli nation-state or the ways its emergence and continuation have relied upon the occupation, expulsion, and disenfranchisement of what are now millions of Palestinians. So PQBDS is not only against the occupation, but is also in favor of the rights of expelled refugees, against past and continuing land confiscation, and opposed to the compromised rights of Palestinians who are partially recognized as citizens of Israel.

So the movement seems to equally and emphatically oppose homophobia and affirm Boycott, Divestment, and Sanctions as the best and largest Palestinian movement at this time. As a result, two frameworks are brought together in a way that is not usually done, especially when the Israeli state and its publicity firms now seek to "sell" Israel as a gay-friendly place. The appeal to lesbian, gay, queer, and transgender people is to come visit and support the Israeli state as a place where they can enjoy enfranchisement. But that appeal does not consider who is enfranchised by that state and who is not, and so to take the bait is, in effect, to be willing to accept a narrow, identitarian version of gay rights, and to reject all alliance with those who are disenfranchised, accepting that one form of enfranchisement is effectively bought through a broader and more pervasive form of disenfranchisement. The Palestinians involved with PQBDS are not "living a contradiction," but rather mobilizing an antagonism in order to articulate a broader set of interdependent relations. They are asking all of us to think about, as you say, the radical insufficiency of social movements that purchase their own claim to a livable life by accepting and becoming part of the reproduction of the unlivable lives of others. Whatever notion of interdependency or equality we are thinking about only comes into being through a concerted action that we can call freedom or resistance, depending on the context and the lexicon. But it also means expanding our affective alliances beyond claims of similitude and community.

20

The university, the humanities, and the book bloc

AA: The corporatization of higher education, which is sweeping round the world, is founded on a conception of knowledge as property, commodity, and a measurable commercial asset that needs to be immediately available to the managerial agendas of global business elites. As universities become accountable to corporate governmentality through regimes of knowledge commercialization, quantitative assessment, auditability, and benchmarking, the humanities and the social sciences (especially those using critical epistemologies) represent a risk, not only economic but also political, since critical thinking is cast as a hazardous surplus to the entrepreneurial university. In a context of marketability and bottom-line efficiency, the humanities are rendered redundant. I am wondering how we might imagine an alternative future for the university in these anti-intellectual times. What kind of critique could be articulated to make sense of and to make a claim for alternative humanities (in both senses of the word: both alternative to "high culture" as essence of humanism and humanity, and as an alternative conceptualization of what counts as human)? It seems to me that we urgently need to recover and reclaim the uncommodifiable unconditionality of the university, although it is worth remembering that universities have always been places of power, hierarchy, inequality, and asymmetrical political economy. So there is a question about what exactly is to be reclaimed here. There is also a question about what kinds of critical scholarship of humanities and post-humanities this reclaiming would require.

As we know, many European and US cities have been recently pulsating with massive protests at their universities, against the cost of tuition, against regimes of university governance, and against the marketization of higher education. One of the most striking modes of protest was arguably the "book bloc," in which protesters marched wearing book shields in the streets of Rome, London, and other cities, in defense of public universities and libraries. The list of the books that have taken part in the book bloc includes: Adorno's *Negative Dialectics*, Virginia Woolf's *A Room of One's Own*, Mary Shelley's *Frankenstein*, Beckett's *Waiting for Godot*, and your *Gender Trouble*. An image that has been circulated among several blogs epitomizes in a remarkably eloquent way, I think, the spirit, or the specter, of our time: a policeman raises his baton against a protester who carries a book sign of Derrida's *Specters of Marx*. This image of an armed policeman chasing the specters of Marx reminds us that those recurring specters still haunt capitalism; it reminds us, above all, that sometimes we have to fight *for* our books, *with* our books.

JB: Of course, in earlier times, so many people would have been critical of books such as Derrida's. Will it give us the tools we need to do politics? Is it sufficiently political? But now there is the pressing question of whether there will be institutional sites where such debates can be had, and whether the opportunity to read books such as Derrida's will still be possible. It may be that knowledge will begin even more radically to circulate outside the university, and though there are many reasons to wish for the displacement of the university as the center for knowledge, it would be an unimaginable loss for the university to become a privatized industry that mainly trains its students for marketable pursuits. Where and when do we engage in any criticism of market values themselves, of the contingent and restrictive model of rationality now traveling under the name of neoliberalism? We are in a terrible conundrum when in order to underscore the importance of critical theory and critical thinking more generally, we have to "prove its marketability." It is unfortunately all too familiar to consider a market argument for betting against the market (that happens all the time), but does critical theory need to analogize itself to betting against the stock market in order to be sustained as a funded dimension of the university? In a way, we are waging a fight over values in a field in which the market seeks to be the only measure of value. My sense is that this is one reason people have taken to the streets. For the problem, as you know, is not only that critical thinking risks becoming unfundable within institutions driven by market values, but that basic rights and entitlements are also eroded within such a context, refashioned as "investments" or as "disposable goods."

In a way, the situation of non-tenured academic workers forms a bridge between the institutional crisis of knowledge and the production of disposable populations. For those who can and will teach the humanities, languages, or critical thinking may well be understood as classes of workers that are substitutable. In the United States the number of academic workers without security of employment has grown exponentially in recent years. And when state law or union regulations demand that non-tenured faculty become eligible for reviews that would establish security of employment, employers very often refuse to renew the contracts, letting workers go right before the moment in which they stand a chance of securing their futures. So we see how universities are actively participating in deciding which population of workers will be disposable, and which will not. And students who are coming up through the university, watching language classes being cut, finding themselves in over-enrolled courses or shut out of their majors, also recognize that their lives and educations are being sacrificed for a set of market calculations. When universities become unaffordable, as is increasingly the case in the United States, we see as well the university as a site that reproduces and hardens rigid class stratifications.

So, do we wonder that students and workers are taking to the streets, finding alliances with one another, and that university buildings are being seized or occupied in an effort to draw media attention to the question: Who can find entry into the halls of the university? Indeed, the questions are many: Who can afford to go? Who can afford to teach there at wages that are not sustaining? And who can afford to live out a life in which one's labor is disposable and the worth of one's knowledge is unrecognizable by prevailing market standards? The result is surely rage, but perhaps we can ask more precisely how to make sense of bodies that assemble on the street, or that occupy buildings, or that find themselves gathering in public squares or along the routes that line the center of cities?

Spaces of appearance, politics of exposure

AA: My sense is that our conversation, Judith, perhaps in its entirety, has been insistently gesturing toward the question – and the affective labor – of critical agency, in its entwinement with multiple forms of doing, undoing, being undone, and becoming, as well as multiple forms of giving and giving up. In seeking to map out a differential and multi-sited topology of radical transformational action, we have dealt with the question of how present regimes of dispossession are displaced into a labor of sensing, imagining, envisaging, and forging an alternative to the present. As we are affected by dispossession, the affect of dispossession is not quite our own. And as we are rendered vulnerable to another's dispossession, or to another dispossession, we engage in a commonality of political resistance and transformative action – albeit not letting our affective alliances cede to claims of similitude and community. And so our main concern has been the processes by which embodied subjects, simultaneously produced and foreclosed via the violence of neo-colonial, capitalist, racial, gendered, and sexualized regulatory schemas, present themselves in their erasure. This is about the challenge of taking into account the politics of precarious and dispossessed subjectivity, in claiming the right and the desire to a political otherwise.

In seeking to make sense of the potentialities of bodies that assemble on the streets and squares of the world, or fight street battles over public education, we can also track how these multi-sited aggregations might serve not to reinsert a nostalgic communitarian politics of place, but rather to displace conventional conceptions of the "public sphere," or the polis, understood as the particular spatial location of political life. The perspective of an affective politics of the performative that we are pursuing here clearly resonates with Arendt's formulation of the "space of appearance"[1] that is brought into being through political action. For our purposes here, we might find it useful to shift from *spaces of appearance* to *spacing appearance*. In this context, the notion of space should by no means be taken as synonymous with fixity, but rather implies a performative plane of "taking place." In this sense, "appearance" is not reducible to a surface phenomenality; rather it opens up to concern what is performed in ways that avow the unperformable. I guess there is a set of questions here: How does "appearance" relate to "spacing," "taking space," and "taking place" when it comes to bodies on the streets? How could appearance relate to exposure – exposure to the violence of the polis but also exposure to others, other places, and other politics?

But if there can be no realm of appearance possible apart from social normativity and thus from imposed invisibleness, the challenge is to mobilize "appearance" without taking for granted its naturalized epistemological premises – visibility, transparency – that have been abundantly used to reify political subjectivity. It is through stabilizing norms of gender, sexuality, nationality, raciality, able-bodiedness, land and capital ownership that subjects are interpellated to fulfill the conditions of possibility for their appearance to be recognized as human. Can "anybody" (any body) appear then? How do particular forms of corporeal engagement become available to the normative cultures of intelligibility, sensibility, and livability? This question of who can appear gets complicated, and occasionally gets into trouble, when a realm of appearance comes face to face with an uncanny stranger whose appearance and claim to public space are taken to yield a dissonance; it also gets complicated when an assembly is faced with the disjunctive performative force of sheer socio-historical specificity. Consider, for example, that the protest encampment at the University of New Mexico is called "(*Un*)occupy Albuquerque" to highlight the fact that the land there is occupied native land. I would say that this is, indeed, a particularly creative dissonance, one that renders the very conceptual grounds of "occupation" accountable to historical difference and thus to its own material conditions of possibility. I think we might think of this openness to possibility as crucial to the desire for the event of radical, agonistic democracy.

JB: In some ways, the question is too large, since there are all kinds of assemblies: the revolutionary assemblies in Tunisia and Egypt, the demonstrations against educational cuts, and against the emerging hegemony of neoliberalism in higher education that we have seen in Athens, Rome, London, Wisconsin, and Berkeley, to name but a few. And then there are the demonstrations that are without immediate demands, such as Occupy Wall Street, and then, of course, there are the riots in the UK, which are also without explicit demands, but the political significance of which cannot be underestimated when we consider the extent of poverty and unemployment among those who were looting. When people take to the streets together, they form something of a body politic, and even if that body politic does not speak in a single voice – even when it does not speak at all – it still forms, asserting its presence as a plural and obdurate bodily life. What is the political significance of assembling as bodies, stopping traffic or claiming attention, or moving not as stray and separated individuals, but as a social movement of some kind? It does not have to be organized from on high (the Leninist presumption), and it does not need to have a single message (the Logocentric conceit), for assembled bodies to exercise a certain performative force in the public domain. The "We are here" that translates that collective bodily presence might be re-read as "We are *still* here," meaning: "We have not yet been disposed of. We have not slipped quietly into the shadows of public life: we have not become the glaring absence that structures your public life." In a way, the collective assembling of bodies is an exercise of the popular will, and a way of asserting, in bodily form, one of the most basic presuppositions of democracy, namely that political and public institutions are bound to represent the people, and to do so in ways that establish equality as a presupposition of social and political existence. So when those institutions become structured in such a way that certain populations become disposable, are interpellated as disposable, deprived of a future, of education, of stable and fulfilling work, of even knowing what one can call a home, then surely the assemblies fulfill another function, not only the expression of justifiable rage, but the assertion in their very social organization of principles of equality. Bodies on the street are precarious – they are exposed to police force and sometimes endure physical suffering as a result. But those bodies are also obdurate and persisting, insisting on their continuing and collective "thereness" and, in these recent forms, organizing themselves without hierarchy, thus exemplifying the principles of equal treatment that they are demanding of public institutions. In this way, those bodies enact a message, performatively, even when they sleep in public, even when they organize collective methods for cleaning the grounds they occupy, as happened in Tahrir Square and on Wall Street. If there is a crowd, there is also a media event that forms across time and space, calling for the demonstrations, so some set of global connections is being articulated, a different sense of the global from the "globalized market." And some set of values is being enacted in the form of a collective resistance: a defense of our collective precarity and persistence in the making of equality and the many-voiced and unvoiced ways of refusing to become disposable.

Notes

Preface

1 "Amfisvitontas to 'Kanoniko,' Anadiamorfonontas to Dynato: Feminismos, Queer Politiki kai Rizospastiki Aristera," in *Epitelestikotita kai Episfaleia: I Judith Butler stin Athina.*
2 *Zoe sto Orio: Dokimia gia to Soma, to Fylo kai ti Viopolitiki.*
3 *I Krisi os "Katastasi Ektaktis Anagkis": Kritikes kai Antistaseis.*
4 See Athena Athanasiou, "Technologies of Humanness, Aporias of Biopolitics, and the Cut Body of Humanity," *differences*, 14(1) (2003): 125–62.

Chapter 1 Aporetic dispossession, or the trouble with dispossession

1 C.B. MacPherson, *The Political Theory of Possessive Individualism: Hobbes to Locke* (Oxford: Clarendon Press, 1962).

Chapter 2 The logic of dispossession and the matter of the human (after the critique of metaphysics of substance)

1 See Edward Said, *The Politics of Dispossession: The Struggle for Palestinian Self-Determination, 1969–1994* (New York: Vintage, 1995). See also Elizabeth Povinelli, "The Child in the Broom Closet: States of Killing and Letting Die," *South Atlantic Quarterly* 107(3) (2008): 509–30.
2 The word *debtocracy* (Greek: hreokratía) is a neologism that implies current neoliberal mutations of democracy and is inspired by the title of a 2011 documentary film by Katerina Kitidi and Aris Hatzistefanou, which offers a critical account of the Greek debt crisis.

3 David Harvey, *The New Imperialism* (Oxford: Oxford University Press, 2003).

4 For an analysis of how the subject who emerges in the colonial context is formed through the co-constitution of raciality and property ownership, see Brenna Bhandar, "Plasticity and Post-Colonial Recognition: 'Owning, Knowing and Being'," *Law and Critique*, 22(3) (2011): 227–49.

5 Jacques Derrida, *Specters of Marx: The State of the Debt, the Work of Mourning and the New International*, trans. Peggy Kamuf (London: Routledge, 1994), p. 126.

6 Ibid.

7 Orlando Patterson, *Slavery and Social Death: A Comparative Study* (Cambridge, MA: Harvard University Press, 1982).

8 Achille Mbembe, "Necropolitics," *Public Culture*, 15(1) (2003): 11–40; Mbembe, *On the Postcolony* (Berkeley: University of California Press, 2001).

9 Ruth Wilson Gilmore, *Golden Gulag: Prisons, Surplus, Crisis, and Opposition in Globalizing California* (Berkeley: University of California Press, 2007).

10 Mbembe, "Necropolitics"; Mbembe, *On the Postcolony*.

11 Rosa Parks with Jim Haskins, Rosa Parks: My Story (New York: Dial Books, 1992), p. 116.

12 Aileen Moreton-Robinson, "I Still Call Australia Home: Indigenous Belonging and Place in a White Postcolonizing Society," in Sara Ahmed, Claudia Castañeda, Anne-Marie Fortier, and Mimi Sheller (eds.), *Uprootings/Regroundings: Questions of Home and Migration* (Oxford: Berg, 2003), pp. 23–40.

13 See also: Brenna Bhandar, "Plasticity and Post-Colonial Recognition: 'Owning, Knowing and Being'," *Law and Critique*, 22(3) (2011): 227–49; Hussein Abu Hussein and Fiona Mackay, *Access Denied: Palestinian Land Rights in Israel* (London: Zed Books, 2003); Eyal Weizman, *Hollow Land: Israel's Architecture of Occupation* (London: Verso, 2007).

14 Oren Yiftachel, *Ethnocracy: Land and Identity Politics in Israel/Palestine* (Philadelphia: University of Pennsylvania Press, 2006).

15 Stewart Motha, "Reconciliation as Domination," in Scott Veitch (ed.), *Law and the Politics of Reconciliation* (Aldershot: Ashgate, 2007), pp. 69–91.

16 Veena Das, *Critical Events: An Anthropological Perspective on Contemporary India* (Oxford: Oxford University Press, 1997).

17 See also Kevin Bales, *Disposable People: New Slavery in the Global Economy* (Berkeley: University of California Press, 1999).

18 Brenna Bhandar, "Plasticity and Post-Colonial Recognition: 'Owning, Knowing and Being'," *Law and Critique*, 22(3) (2011): 227–49.

19 Ranjana Khanna's introduction of the category of disposability is valuable in its critically refining Giorgio Agamben's notion of "bare life" through focusing on the gendered colonized subject. See Ranjana Khanna, "Disposability," *differences*, 20(1) (2009): 181–98.

20 For an insightful discussion of this problematic in light of the failures and limits of the dialectic of recognition in the Canadian context, see Brenna

Bhandar, "Plasticity and Post-Colonial Recognition: 'Owning, Knowing and Being,'" *Law and Critique*, 22(3) (2011): 227–49.

21 Michel Foucault, "The Ethics of the Concern for Self as a Practice of Freedom," in Michel Foucault, *Ethics, Subjectivity and Truth*, Vol. 1 of *Essential Works of Foucault 1954–1984*, ed. Paul Rabinow (New York: The New Press, 1997), pp. 281–301.

22 Michel Foucault, *Society Must Be Defended*, trans. David Macey (New York: Picador, 2002).

23 Ann Stoler, *Carnal Knowledge and Imperial Power: Race and the Intimate in Colonial Rule* (Berkeley: University of California Press, 2002).

24 Lauren Berlant, *Cruel Optimism*. Durham: Duke University Press, 2011.

25 Elizabeth Povinelli, *Economies of Abandonment: Social Belonging and Endurance in Late Liberalism* (Durham, NC: Duke University Press, 2011).

26 Theodor Adorno, *Minima Moralia: Reflections from Damaged Life*, trans. E. F. Jephcott (London: Verso, 1996).

27 Samera Esmeir, *Juridical Humanity: A Colonial History* (Stanford: Stanford University Press, 2012).

Chapter 3 A caveat about the "primacy of economy"

1 See also the exchange between Judith Butler and Nancy Fraser in *New Left Review* and *Social Text* for different views on the relationship between capitalism and heterosexism: Judith Butler, "Merely Cultural," *New Left Review*, 227 (January–February 1998): 33–44 (previously published in *Social Text*, 52/53 [Fall–Winter 1997]: 265–76); Nancy Fraser, "Heterosexism, Misrecognition and Capitalism: A Response to Judith Butler," *New Left Review*, 228 (March–April 1998): 140–50 (previously published in *Social Text*, 52/53 [Fall–Winter 1997]: 279–89).

2 Wendy Brown, "Neo-liberalism and the End of Liberal Democracy," *Theory and Event*, 7(1) (2003) (online journal).

Chapter 4 Sexual dispossessions

1 Leticia Sabsay, *Las normas del deseo* (Madrid: Ediciones Catedra, 2009), pp. 119–28.

2 See Eve Kosofsky Sedgwick, *Epistemology of the Closet* (Berkeley: University of California Press, 1990).

3 Joseph A. Massad, *Desiring Arabs* (Chicago: University of Chicago Press, 2007).

4 See also Jasbir Puar, *Terrorist Assemblages: Homonationalism in Queer Times* (Durham, NC: Duke University Press, 2007).

5 Judith Butler, *Bodies That Matter: On the Discursive Limits of "Sex"* (London and New York: Routledge, 1993), p. 91.

6 Eve Kosofsky Sedgwick, "Paranoid Reading and Reparative Reading; or, You're So Paranoid You Probably Think This Essay Is About You," in *Touching Feeling: Affect, Pedagogy, Performativity* (Durham, NC: Duke University Press, 2003), pp. 123–51.

Chapter 5 (Trans)possessions, or bodies beyond themselves

1 Marilyn Strathern, *The Gender of the Gift: Problems with Women and Problems with Society in Melanesia* (Berkeley: University of California Press, 1988). See also Henrietta Moore, *The Subject of Anthropology: Gender, Symbolism and Psychoanalysis* (Cambridge: Polity Press, 2007).
2 The script of the film was written in 2004–5.
3 Judith Butler, "Quandaries of the Incest Taboo," in *Undoing Gender* (New York: Routledge, 2004), pp. 152–60 (p. 154).
4 Jane Gallop, *The Daughter's Seduction: Feminism and Psychoanalysis* (Ithaca, NY: Cornell University Press, 1984).

Chapter 6 The sociality of self-poietics: Talking back to the violence of recognition

1 *Eleftherotypia*, January 25, 2009.
2 See Wendy Brown, *Regulating Aversion: Tolerance in the Age of Identity and Empire* (Princeton: Princeton University Press, 2006).
3 Michel Foucault, "What is Critique?" in *The Politics of Truth* (Los Angeles: Semiotext(e), 1997), pp. 41–82.
4 Ewa Plonowska Ziarek, *An Ethics of Dissensus: Postmodernity, Feminism, and the Politics of Radical Democracy* (Stanford: Stanford University Press, 2001).
5 Adriana Cavarero, *For More Than One Voice: Toward a Philosophy of Vocal Expression*, trans. Paul A. Kottman (Stanford: Stanford University Press, 2005).

Chapter 7 Recognition and survival, or surviving recognition

1 Elizabeth Povinelli, *The Cunning of Recognition: Indigenous Alterities and the Making of Australian Multiculturalism* (Durham, NC: Duke University Press, 2002), p. 108.
2 Gayatri Chakravorty Spivak, *Outside in the Teaching Machine* (New York: Routledge, 1993), pp. 45–6.
3 Frantz Fanon, *Black Skin, White Masks*, trans. Constance Farrington (New York: Grove Press, 1994).
4 Ibid., p. 232.
5 Ibid., p. 231.
6 Jacques Rancière, *Disagreement: Politics and Philosophy*, trans. Julie Rose (Minneapolis: University of Minnesota Press, 2004).
7 Judith Butler and Gayatri Chakravorty Spivak, *Who Sings the Nation-State? Language, Politics, Belonging* (London: Seagull Books, 2007).
8 Wendy Brown, *States of Injury: Power and Freedom in Late Modernity* (Princeton: Princeton University Press, 1995).
9 Similarly, Patchen Markell has argued that conceptualizing sociality and social identity in terms of reciprocal recognition fortifies identity-based

injustices. Patchen Markell, *Bound by Recognition* (Princeton: Princeton University Press, 2003).

10 See Jacques Derrida, "Force of Law: The Mystical Foundation of Authority," trans. Mary Quaintance, *Cardozo Law Review*, 11(5–6) (1990): 921–1045.

Chapter 10 Responsiveness as responsibility

1 See Michel Feher, "Self-Appreciation; or, The Aspirations of Human Capital," *Public Culture* 21(1) (2009): 21–41.

2 G. W. F. Hegel, *Natural Law: The Scientific Ways of Treating Natural Law, Its Place in Moral Philosophy, and Its Relation to the Positive Sciences of Law*, trans. T. M. Knox (Philadelphia: University of Pennsylvania Press, 1975).

3 Didier Fassin and Richard Rechtman, *The Empire of Trauma: An Inquiry into the Condition of Victimhood* (Princeton: Princeton University Press, 2009). Mariella Pandolfi, "L'industrie humanitaire: Une souveraineté mouvante et supracoloniale: Réflexion sur l'expérience des Balkans," *Multitudes* 3 (2000): 97–105. See also Didier Fassin and Mariella Pandolfi (eds.), *Contemporary States of Emergency: The Politics of Military and Humanitarian Interventions* (New York: Zone Books, 2010).

4 See Didier Fassin and Estelle D' Halluin, "The Truth from the Body: Medical Certificates as Ultimate Evidence for Asylum Seekers," *American Anthropologist*, 107(4) (2005): 597–608.

5 See Kathleen Woodward, "Calculating Compassion," in Lauren Berlant (ed.), *Compassion: The Culture and Politics of an Emotion* (New York: Routledge, 2004), pp. 59–86.

6 Lee Edelman, "Compassion's Compulsion," in Berlant (ed.), *Compassion*, pp. 159–86.

7 Jean-Luc Nancy, *The Inoperative Community*, ed. Peter Connor (Minneapolis: University of Minnesota Press, 1991). See also Nancy, *Being Singular Plural*, trans. Robert Richardson and Anne O'Byrne (Stanford: Stanford University Press, 2000).

8 Judith Butler, *Precarious Life: The Powers of Mourning and Violence* (London: Verso, 2004), p. 33.

9 Wendy Brown, *Regulating Aversion: Tolerance in the Age of Identity and Empire* (Princeton: Princeton University Press, 2006).

10 See Jacques Derrida, "Force of Law: The Mystical Foundation of Authority," trans. Mary Quaintance, *Cardozo Law Review*, 11(5–6) (1990): 921–1045.

11 Hannah Arendt, *Eichmann in Jerusalem: A Report on the Banality of Evil* (New York: Viking Press, 1963).

12 Hannah Arendt, *The Origins of Totalitarianism* (San Diego and New York: Harcourt, 1973).

13 See also Talal Asad, *On Suicide Bombing* (New York: Columbia University Press, 2007), where Asad questions the common western perception of the suicide fighter as the icon of an Islamic culture of death.

14 Ibid.

Chapter 11 Ex-propriating the performative

1 Judith Butler, *Gender Trouble: Feminism and the Subversion of Identity* (London: Routledge, 1990), p. xxvi.
2 Jean-Luc Nancy, *Hegel: The Restlessness of the Negative*, trans. Jason Smith and Steven Miller (Minneapolis: University of Minnesota Press, 2002).
3 Franz Kafka, "Before the Law," in Nahum N. Glatzer (ed.), *Franz Kafka: The Complete Stories and Parables*, trans. Willa and Edwin Muir (New York: Quality Paperback Book Club, 1971), pp. 3–4.
4 Jacques Derrida, "Before the Law," trans. Avital Ronell and Christine Roulton, in *Acts of Literature*, ed. Derek Attridge (New York: Routledge, 1992), pp. 181–220.
5 Jacques Derrida, *Limited Inc.*, trans. Jeffrey Mehlman and Samuel Weber (Evanston, IL: Northwestern University Press, 1988); Derrida, "Before the Law."

Chapter 12 Dispossessed languages, or singularities named and renamed

1 Gayatri Chakravorty Spivak, "Can the Subaltern Speak?" in Cary Nelson and Lawrence Grossberg (eds), *Marxism and the Interpretation of Culture* (Urbana: University of Illinois Press, 1988), pp. 271–313. See also Rosalind Morris (ed.), *Can the Subaltern Speak? Reflections on the History of an Idea* (New York: Columbia University Press, 2010).
2 Adriana Cavarero, *Horrorism: Naming Contemporary Violence* (New York: Columbia University Press, 2009).
3 Jean-Luc Nancy, *Being Singular Plural*, trans. Robert Richardson and Anne O'Byrne (Stanford: Stanford University Press, 2000).
4 As Derrida explains (*Politics of Friendship*, trans. George Collins, London: Verso, 1997, pp. 46–7, fn. 15), these words of Bataille's are chosen by Blanchot as an epigraph to *The Unavowable Community* (trans. Pierre Joris, Tarrytown, NY: Station Hill Press, 1988), a book which converses with an article by Jean-Luc Nancy which later became the book *The Inoperative Community* (ed. Peter Connor, Minneapolis: University of Minnesota Press, 1991).
5 Derrida, *Politics of Friendship*, p. 35.
6 Hannah Arendt, *The Origins of Totalitarianism* (San Diego and New York: Harcourt, 1973), p. 455.

Chapter 13 The political promise of the performative

1 See also Ranjana Khanna, "Disposability," *differences* 20(1) (2009), 181–98.
2 Eve Kosofsky Sedgwick, "How to Bring Your Kids Up Gay," *Social Text* 29 (1991): 18–27.
3 Several women's groups have been formed to protest official indifference, such as "Nuestras Hijas de Regreso a Casa" ("Civil Association for the Return Home of Our Daughters"). In November 2001, "Las Mujeres de

Negro" ("Women in Black") protested on the day of celebration of the
Mexican Revolution in the city of Chihuahua.

4 Achille Mbembe, "Necropolitics," *Public Culture*, 15(1) (2003): 11–40;
Mbembe, *On the Postcolony* (Berkeley: University of California Press,
2001).

5 Lauren Berlant, *Cruel Optimism* (Durham, NC: Duke University Press,
2011).

Chapter 14 The governmentality of "crisis" and its resistances

1 Judith Butler, Ernesto Laclau, and Slavoj Žižek, *Contingency, Hegemony, Universality: Contemporary Dialogues on the Left* (London: Verso, 2000),
p. 268.

Chapter 15 Enacting another vulnerability: On owing and owning

1 Judith Butler, *Undoing Gender* (New York: Routledge, 2004), p. 231.

2 Elspeth Probyn, *Outside Belongings* (New York: Routledge, 1996); Vikki
Bell (ed.), *Performativity and Belonging* (London: Sage, 1999); Ranjana
Khanna, "Unbelonging: In motion," *differences*, 21(1) (2010): 109–23.

Chapter 16 Trans-border affective foreclosures and state racism

1 Achille Mbembe, "Necropolitics," *Public Culture*, 15(1) (2003): 11–40;
Mbembe, *On the Postcolony* (Berkeley: University of California Press,
2001).

2 Lauren Berlant, "Slow Death (Sovereignty, Obesity, Lateral Agency)," *Critical Inquiry*, 33(4) (2007): 754–79. See also Berlant, *Cruel Optimism*
(Durham, NC: Duke University Press, 2011).

3 Ibid.

Chapter 18 The political affects of plural performativity

1 Michel Foucault, "The Subject and Power," in Hubert Dreyfus and Paul
Rabinow, *Michel Foucault: Beyond Structuralism and Hermeneutics*
(Chicago: University of Chicago Press, 1982), pp. 221–2.

Chapter 21 Spaces of appearance, politics of exposure

1 Hannah Arendt, *The Human Condition* (Chicago: University of Chicago
Press, 1958), pp. 198–9.

Index

Index

Index

Index